CW01373493

PESTS & DISEASES OF FRUIT TREES & SHRUBS

Copyright © C. Thornton 2014

The right of C. Thornton to be identified as the author of this work has been asserted in accordance with the Copyright, Designs and Patents Act, 1988.

All rights reserved. No part of this book may be reproduced or transmitted by any person or entity (including Google, Amazon or similar organisations) in any form or by any means, electronic or mechanical, including photocopying, recording or by any information storage and retrieval system, without prior permission in writing from the publisher.

National Library of Australia Cataloguing-in-Publication entry

Creator: Thornton, C., author.

Title: Pests and diseases of fruit trees and shrubs / C. Thornton.

ISBN: 9781925110609 (paperback)

Series: Rare and heritage fruit ; Set 2, no. 8.

Notes: Includes index.

Subjects: Plant diseases--Australia.
Fruit--Diseases and pests--Australia.
Shrubs--Diseases and pests--Australia.

Dewey Number: 6320994

LEAVES of GOLD PRESS ®

ABN 67 099 575 078

PO Box 9113, Brighton, 3186, Victoria, Australia
www.leavesofgoldpress.com

RARE AND HERITAGE FRUIT
GROWING #8

PESTS & DISEASES OF FRUIT TREES & SHRUBS

C. Thornton
Edited by Laura C. A. Walker

- RARE AND HERITAGE FRUIT -
THE SERIES

SET #1
RARE AND HERITAGE FRUIT
- CULTIVARS -

1 Apples
2 Cider Apples
3 Crabapples
4 European Pears
5 Nashi Pears
6 Perry Pears
7 Apricots
8 Peaches
9 Nectarines
10 European Plums
11 Japanese Plums
12 Cherries
13 Figs
14 Cactus & Dragon Fruits
15 Oranges
16 Lemons
17 Limes

18 Mandarins & Grapefruit
19 Kumquats, Calamondins & Chinottos
20 Rare & Unusual Citrus
21 Nuts
22 Berries & Small Fruits
23 Quinces
24 Guavas & Feijoas
25 Table Grapes
26 Wine Grapes
27 Avocados
28 Rare & Unusual Fruits

and more...

SET #2
RARE AND HERITAGE FRUIT
- GROWING -

1 Propagating Fruit Plants (other than grafting)
2 Grafting and Budding Fruit Trees
3 Planting Fruit Trees and Shrubs
4 Care of Fruit Trees (compost, mulch, water etc)
5 Pruning Fruit Trees and Shrubs
6 Training and Espaliering Fruit Trees and Shrubs
7 Harvesting and Storage of Fruit
8 Pests and Diseases of Fruit Trees and Shrubs

SET #3
RARE AND HERITAGE FRUIT
- PRESERVING -

1 Fruit Preserving (drying, crystallizing, bottling etc.)
2 Cider Making
3 Perry Making ('pear cider')
4 Fruit Wine Making
5 Fruit Spirits and Liqueurs Making
6 Fruit Schnapps Making

www.leavesofgoldpress.com

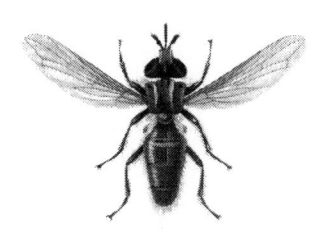

RARE AND HERITAGE FRUIT[1]

This book is one of a series written for 'backyard farmers' of the 21st century. The series focuses on rare and heritage fruit in Australia, although it includes much information of interest to fruit enthusiasts in every country.

For the purpose of this series, rare fruits are species neither indigenous to nor commercially cultivated in any given region.

'Heritage' or 'heirloom' fruits such as old-fashioned varieties[2] of apple, quince, fig, plum, peach and pear are increasingly popular due to their diverse flavors, excellent nutritional qualities and other desirable characteristics.

It is much easier for modern supermarkets to offer only a limited range of fruit cultivars (i.e. varieties) to consumers, instead of dozens of different kinds of apples, pears etc. During the 19th and early 20th centuries, however, the diversity was huge. Old nursery catalogues were filled with numerous named varieties of fruits, nuts and berries, few of which are available these days.

What are heritage fruits? 'An heirloom plant, heirloom variety, heritage fruit (Australia), or (especially in the UK) heirloom vegetable

---

1   Note: this introduction is identical in every handbook in the Rare and Heritage Fruit series.
2   The correct term in this case is 'cultivars'; however most people are more familiar with the term 'varieties' and although it is not strictly accurate, we use the terms interchangeably in this series.

is an old cultivar that is 'still maintained by gardeners and farmers particularly in isolated or ethnic communities'.[3]

'These may have been commonly grown during earlier periods in human history, but are not used in modern large-scale agriculture. Many heirloom vegetables have kept their traits through open pollination, while fruit varieties such as apples have been propagated over the centuries through grafts and cuttings.'[4]

Broadly speaking, heritage fruits are historic cultivars; those which have initially been selected or bred by human beings and given officially recognized names, before being propagated by successive generations of growers, retaining their genetic integrity far beyond the normal life-span of an individual plant; those which are not protected by a private plant-breeders' licence, but instead belong to the public at large. They are the legacy of our ancestors; living heirlooms; part of humanity's horticultural, vintage and culinary heritage.

Fruit enthusiasts around the globe are currently reviving our horticultural legacy by renovating old orchards and identifying rare, historic fruit varieties. The goal is to make a much wider range of fruit trees available again to the home gardener.

This series of handbooks aims to help.

STORIES

Like people, every fruit cultivar has a name and a story. Take the Granny Smith apple, for example - the most successful Australian apple, instantly identifiable with its smooth green skin, exported world-wide, and now cultivated in numerous countries.

This famous cultivar began in the 1860s as a tiny seedling that chanced to spring up in a compost heap. An orchardist by the name of Mrs Maria Ann Smith lived with her ailing husband in Eastwood, New South Wales (now a suburb of Sydney). She was in her late sixties, a hard worker and the mother of many children.

One autumn day, as usual, Maria Smith drove her horse-drawn wagon home from the Sydney markets, where she had been selling the

---

3   Whealy, K. (1990). 'Seed Savers Exchange: preserving our genetic heritage'.(Transactions of the Illinois State Horticultural Society 123: 80–84.)

4   'Heirloom plants' Wikipedia, accessed October 2013

fruit from her orchard. The wagon possibly contained a few wooden crates she had purchased after selling her produce, in which to transport the next load of wares. One or two leftover Tasmanian-grown French Crab apples might still have been lying in the crates, somewhat battered and past their prime. Imagine 'Granny' Smith, her gray hair tucked up inside her bonnet, trudging down to the creek from which the household drew its water and dumping their decaying remains on its banks.

There in that damp spot, sinking into compost-rich soil, the apple pips lay throughout the winter months. Come spring, one of them split open and a tiny white rootlet appeared. It swiftly bored downwards, stood up and threw off its black seed-case, revealing two perfect, green cotyledons.

The leaves quickly multiplied as the seedling grew, Maria spied it next time she walked down to the creek, the hems of her long black skirts rustling through the ferns. She nurtured the infant tree until it grew up and bore fruit. When at last she picked the first green-skinned apple and took a bite, she must have been surprised by the crisp, hard flesh and sharp taste. No doubt she used it to make pies and other desserts for her sick husband and numerous grand-children, thus discovering that this new cultivar was good for both cooking and eating.

She shared the apples with friends and neighbours, allowing them to cut scion-wood from her tree and graft their own cloned versions. Locally, word of the apple's qualities spread.

'Smith died only a couple years after her discovery, but dozens of Granny Smith apple trees lived on in her neighbours' orchards. Her new cultivar did not receive widespread attention until, in 1890, it was exhibited as 'Smith's Seedling' at the Castle Hill Agricultural and Horticultural Show. The following year it won the prize for cooking apples under the name 'Granny Smith's Seedling'.

'The apple became a hit. In 1895 the New South Wales Department of Agriculture officially recognized the cultivar and began growing it at the Government Experimental Station in Bathurst, New South Wales, recommending its properties as a late-picking cooking apple for potential export.

'During the first half of the 20th century the government actively promoted the apple, leading to its widespread acceptance. However, its worldwide fame grew from the fact that it was such a good 'keeper'. Because of its excellent shelf life the Granny Smith could be transported over long distances in cold storage and in most seasons. Granny Smiths were exported in enormous quantities after the First World War, and by 1975 forty percent of Australia's apple crop was Granny Smiths. By this time the apple was being grown extensively elsewhere in the southern hemisphere, as well as in France, Great Britain and the United States.'

'The advent of the Granny Smith Apple is now celebrated annually in Eastwood with the Granny Smith Festival.[5]

Fruit cultivar stories continue to arise in the 21st century. From AAP, February 21, 2010, 'Mudgee Farmer Bruce Davis Creates New Fruit':

'Is it a plum? Is it a peach? It's probably a pleach as it's a morph of the two tasty stonefruits. Whatever it is, it's a love child of the two, accidentally created by a retired NSW farmer.

'Bruce Davis from Mudgee in the state's central west couldn't believe it when he discovered he had grown a cross between a peach and a plum. The fruit looks like a peach from the outside, but resembles a red plum when bitten into. 'The unusual fruit is believed to be the first of its kind ever grown in the state.

'Mr Davis grows peach and blood plum trees alongside each other and believes the peach/plum tree may have grown from compost that contained plum seeds.

"It's a really interesting piece of fruit and it's very tasty," Mr Davis said.

'A cross between a plum and an apricot, known as a pluot, has been grown in the past, but a peach and a plum is a new combination for NSW, Primary Industries Minister Steve Whan said.

'Industry and Investment NSW Mudgee horticulturist Susan Marte said this was the first time she had heard of anyone accidentally crossing the two fruits.'

---

[5] *'Granny Smith Festival'*. Wikipedia, accessed October 2013

NAMES

The origins of the Mudgee pleach and the Granny Smith apple are two of many intriguing fruit stories, but sometimes the name - or names - of cultivars tells yet another story, an etymological one. Names may be inspired by the place a new cultivar was discovered, by the person who selected or bred it, by the shape, flavor, color or use of the fruit, by an event that took place around the time of discovery, by somebody's sweetheart, or any number of other factors.

Names, too, may be multiplied.

The Granny Smith apple was discovered after the advent of newspapers. If you forgot what the prize-winning cultivar was called, you could look it up and there it would be, in black and white. This was not the case for many ancient cultivars.

The Granny Smith apple's probable mother, the French Crab, itself boasts twenty-six listed synonyms, probably invented by forgetful apple-growers.

Another instance of numerous synonyms is the French cider apple whose name is Calville Rouge D'Hiver, meaning 'Calville Winter Red'. It arose in the late 1500s, and as its popularity spread across Europe, the first thing that happened was that people translated the name into their own language: 'Teli Piros Kalvil', 'Roter Winter Calville, 'Calvilla Rossa di Pasqua', 'Cerveny Zimni Hranac' etc.

Next, when absent-minded peasants could not remember the name of this excellent red fruit, they gave it another one. Imagine a weather-beaten farmer in some isolated French village scratching his beard and musing, 'It was something to do with 'Calville'. 'Calville Rouge,' perchance?' Across the valley in another village, a cider-brewer was knitting his (or her) puzzled brow and saying, 'It was something to do with winter, I am thinking, or was it autumn? 'Pomme d'Automne'?' Further afield, a third Frenchman shrugged his shoulders and declared, 'Devil take me if I can remember how it is called, but it is big and red like the heart of a bull, so let us name it "Coeur de Boeuf'."

Fanciful, perhaps, but this might explain why, on the database of the UK's National Fruit Collection, there are more than a hundred synonyms listed for Calville Rouge D'Hiver.

Words are forever evolving. Even when cultivar names stay the same, the language around them is changing and their original meaning becomes lost in the mists of time.

One example of this is the grape cultivar Cabernet Sauvignon, which is considered a relatively new variety, being the product of a chance 17th century crossing between Cabernet franc and Sauvignon blanc.

'Cabernet franc' can be etymologically traced back to 'French Black Grape' (from the Latin word 'caput' which means 'black vine'). The word 'Sauvignon' is believed to be derived from the French 'sauvage', meaning 'wild' and to refer to the grape being a wild grapevine native to France. 'Blanc,' of course, means 'white'. 'Cabernet Sauvignon' no longer means 'Wild Black Grape' in modern French - that would translate as something like 'Vigne Noir Sauvage'. The ancient cultivar name has now taken on its own meaning and is virtually synonymous with the wine made from it.

It is interesting to compare typical cider apple names with, say, typical peach or perry pear names. French words abound among heritage cider apple cultivars, reflecting their roots in medieval Normandy. To the ears of English-speakers these names may sound rather mysterious and aristocratic, until you translate them: for example, Gros Bois, Jaune de Vitré, Moulin à Vent du Calvados, Noël des Champs, Belle Fille de la Manche, Petite Sorte du Parc Dufour and Groin D'âne translate respectively as Big Wood, Yellow Glass, Windmill of Calvados, Christmas Field, Beautiful Girl of the English Channel, Small Kind of Park of the Oven and Donkey's Groin.

Some names of heritage perry pears give us an insight into the bawdy, rustic humour of the perry-drinking English peasants who originally selected them; Ram's Cods, Startle Cock and Bloody Bastard to mention a few.

Heritage grape cultivars have names that come from all over Europe, particularly France and Italy.

Figs go back even further. Humans were cultivating them around 9400 BC, a thousand years before wheat and rye were domesticated. Their names, in English at least, are often drawn from their color and their place of origin - Brown Turkey, White Adriatic, Black Genoa, Pink Jerusalem, Green Ischia ...

Peaches, a more 'modern' fruit in terms of their popularity and breeding, often bear invented names with fancy spellings, such as Florda Glo, Earligrande, Harbrite and Dixigem.

'IMMORTAL' DNA

Another major difference between stonefruit and fruits such as grapes, figs and apples is their ability to grow 'true' to their parents from seed. Stonefruits are far more homozygous than their ancient cousins the pomes (apples, pears etc.) and the grapes. Growers do graft them, but if you plant their seeds the new tree will bear fruit that's fairly similar to that of the parent tree. This means that the centuries-old grafting traditions, the fierce cherishing, the careful bequeathing and the meticulous labelling that accompany pome fruits, grapes and other heterozygotes are not seen as often in the world of peaches and nectarines. This is why many of their cultivar names seem so different, arising as they do from highly organised commercial breeding programmes of the 20th and 21st centuries.

Unlike the seedlings of say, peaches and nectarines, seedling apples are an example of 'extreme heterozygotes', in that rather than inheriting DNA from their parents to create a new apple with those characteristics, they are instead significantly different from their parents.'[6] (Humans are rather like apples in that way, though not as extreme.)

Returning to our green-skinned Australian apple - 'Because the Granny Smith is a chance (and rare) mutation, its seeds tend to produce trees whose fruit have a much less appealing taste. To preserve

---

6   John Lloyd and John Mitchinson (2006). QI: The Complete First Series – QI Factoids

the exact genetic code of any plant variety, a stick of the wood has to be 'cloned'. It has to be grafted onto new roots (or planted directly into the ground, but this is uncommon for trees). Thus, all the Granny Smith apple trees grown today are cuttings of cuttings of cuttings from the original Smith tree in Sydney.'[7]

Cloning by grafting means that the heritage trees - and shrubs - which have survived through the years are genetically identical to their ancestors. Indeed, the heritage plants of today possess exactly the same genetic code as the original trees that arose centuries ago in Asia and Europe. For example, another heritage apple cultivar, 'Court Pendu Plat', is thought to be 1500 years old - the oldest one in existence. Introduced into Europe during Roman times, the living wood from that same tree flourishes to this day, right here in the Great Southern Land.

RARE AND HERITAGE FRUIT IN AUSTRALIA

Many of the rare and heritage fruits that exist in Australia today are clonally descended from plants brought to our shores by the early European settlers, when few, if any, quarantine laws existed. Good luck rather than good stock monitoring limited the number of plant diseases unintentionally imported during the early days of colonization. Fortunately, by 1879 it was recognized that in order to prevent the introduction of serious pests and diseases, quarantine measures were needed. In 1908, the Commonwealth Quarantine service came into operation and took over local quarantine stations in every Australian state.

However, before 1879, there was no limit to the varieties of fruiting plants that could be imported into this country. Many of those old genetic lines survive to this day but sadly, many others have been lost.

Fortunately, Australia is one of only two countries free of fire blight, a serious and ineradicable disease that wiped out millions of apple, pear, loquat and quince trees in Europe and the USA during the 1900s. This means that when certain heritage cultivars went extinct elsewhere, they remained safe in this country. Some have now been restored to their region of origin, now grafted onto fire blight-resistant rootstock.

---

7   *Stirzaker, Richard (2010). Out of the Scientist's Garden: A Story of Water and Food. Collingwood, VIC: CSIRO Pub.*

Over the course of the decades since 1879 Australian fruit growers imported (through quarantine) the latest new cultivars bred by overseas agricultural research stations. Year by year, as scientific advances in breeding and genetics were made, the older cultivars fell out of fashion and were swept aside in favour of the new. They, too, became part of our almost forgotten fruit inheritance.

COMMERCIAL CULTIVARS

Naturally, plant breeders strive to provide the products demanded by the market. Commercial orchardists want to purchase heavy-bearing trees with high disease resistance, whose fruit ripens all at the same time to save on picking costs. Wholesalers want fruit that keeps in storage for a long time without spoiling, and can be shipped without damage. Only firm-fleshed, bruise-resistant fruit will survive modern-day processing. After harvesting, apples, for instance, are tipped into crates, then passed along a conveyor belt through machinery that washes and brushes them clean of insecticides and dirt. This process removes some of the fruit's natural protective coating, so the machines re-apply a commercial grade wax before polishing them to a high shine and pasting a plastic label onto each one. Then the apples are packed into cartons for shipping to markets and stores.

Supermarket shoppers demand visually attractive fruit - large, regular in shape, unblemished and with highly colored skin. Consumers also choose fruit with extra sugar content and juiciness.

All these characteristics, nonetheless, do not necessarily give rise to the best flavor or nutrition. To pick a tree-ripened fruit from your own back yard and bite into it is to experience the taste of fresh food as our forefathers knew it. Growing and preserving their own food, unconcerned with transportability and long storage times, they aimed for a wide variety of fruits, each of which had a unique and delicious taste.

Rare fruit, heritage and heirloom fruit enthusiasts across the world are reviving our horticultural legacy by renovating old orchards and sourcing 'lost' historic and unusual fruit varieties. Their goal is to encourage community participation and to make a wide range of fruit trees available again to the home gardener.

This series of handbooks aims to help.

WHY PRESERVE RARE AND HERITAGE FRUIT?

- They provide access to a wider range of unique and delicious flavors.
- We can enjoy the nutritional benefits of fresh, tree-ripened food.
- Biodiversity: The preservation of a wide range of vital genetic material helps to insure against the ravages of pests and diseases in the future.
- They allow a longer harvesting season, with early and late ripening.
- Culture: heritage varieties, with their interesting assortment of names, are living history.

**Collections of heritage fruit trees are precious.
Anyone who is the custodian of an old tree should treasure it.**

CONTENTS

Rare and Heritage Fruit ix
Introduction 1
1: General Fruit Pests and Diseases 3
2: Apples and Crabapples 55
3: Avocados 67
4. Bananas 69
5. Berries 83
6. Cactus Fruits 97
7. Citrus Fruits 101
8. Figs 119
9. Grapes 125
10. Guavas 143
11. Nuts 147
12. Pawpaws 169

13 Pears 173
14 Stonefruit 181
15 Quinces 191
16 Beneficial Predators 195
17 Pest and Disease Remedies 205
Fruit Care Almanac -Winter 221
Fruit Care Almanac -Winter - Spring 229
Fruit Care Almanac - Summer 239
Fruit Care Almanac - Fall/Autumn 252
Index 261

INTRODUCTION

Growing fruit in your own backyard or home orchard is a real pleasure. The benefits are enormous. You can have access to in-season fruit picked fresh from the tree or shrub, with zero transport miles, rare and unusual varieties with a greater nutritional variety, and delicious fruit flavors all year round. Furthermore, your health will benefit if you get out into the fresh air and sunshine of the garden.

Pests and diseases will inevitably appear at some point in the gardening year, but they need not spoil the enjoyment of growing your own food. There are many useful and chemical-free ways of managing them - including encouraging birds and ladybugs to come and eat the insect pests!

We hope you will enjoy using this book to make your fruit-full garden thrive, and your harvest increase.

1

GENERAL FRUIT PESTS AND DISEASES

Some pests and diseases affect a wide range of fruits.

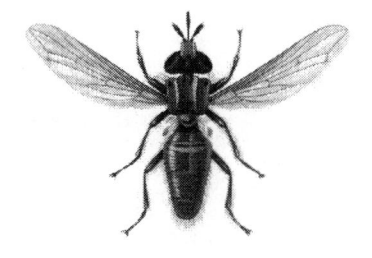

ANTHRACNOSE

Anthracnose is a fungus that attacks a variety of fruit, vegetables and trees. It thrives in warm and humid conditions and is therefore most common in coastal areas in tropical and subtropical conditions. Wet-weather flowering of the avocado can lead to the development of this fungal disease, which attacks the cell walls of the plant, causing growing spots of rotting, infected tissue.

Signs of Infestation

Anthracnose is signified by darkened and sunken lesions occurring on the fruit, flowers, leaves and stems of the plant. Infected leaves exhibit small brown and black spots, which will grow and merge together to form a larger dark spot around which the rest of the leaf will yellow.

The tips of young twigs may also be affected and die back. Infected fruit develop small sunken spots which spread and develop pink spore masses in the centers before starting to rot. Ultimately, affected leaves and fruit will drop off the tree, which means anthracnose has the potential to cause severe defoliation and crop loss.

Organic Control Methods

- You can protect your trees from anthracnose by spreading potash around the base of the tree, before flowering time. Potash acts to thicken the cell walls of the plant, which makes it more difficult for the disease to take hold.

- Make all transplants are healthy. Ideally, chose plants that are resistant to the disease.

- Ensure that the soil is well drained and enriched with compost.

- Watering the plants using a drip sprinkler (instead of an overhead sprinkler or hose) reduces the likelihood of the fungal disease being spread from the ground to the leaves via 'splashback'. With that in mind, avoid touching the wet plants, in case you inadvertently spread the disease.

- Prevent ripening fruits from touching the soil by pruning or tying branches back.

- Every two or three years, rotate your plants.

- If one of your plants does contract anthracnose, remove and destroy all infected parts of the plant. For small fruiting shrubs or vegetables that may unfortunately involve destroying the entire plant. For trees, removing all infected leaves and fruit, and pruning the infected branches and dead wood is sufficient. Make sure all infected plant matter is destroyed well away from the living plant.

- A copper based fungicide will also help control this disease, although it should be used sparingly as excess copper in the soil can be toxic to beneficial microbes and worms.

- Trees may be sprayed with Bordeaux mixture during dormancy.

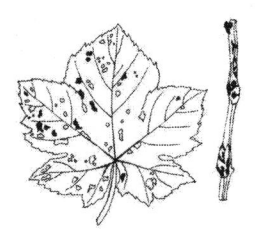

BIRDS

While many birds are gardeners' friends, helping to control insects, fruit-eating birds can be a fruit-grower's bane.

Signs of Infestation

You'll see birds in your fruit trees during the day. They may peck at fruit that is still hanging from the branches, hollowing it out with their sharp beaks. Often, partly-eaten fruit will drop to the ground. Birds prefer ripe fruit but if they are hungry they will peck at it before it is ripe.

Organic Control Methods

* Hanging a fake owl from the tree, suspending CDs or other shiny objects and setting up a scarecrow are all techniques that gardeners have tried for generations to keep birds from their crops, with varying degrees of success. The two main problems associated with these methods are that either the birds tend to become accustomed to the 'scary' object; or that if it is successful in scaring them away, it may also keep beneficial insect-eating birds from the garden.

* Small fruit trees (usually ones less than 2m high) can be protected with bird netting. The downsides to this method include the netting's lack of reusability; the fact leaves can get stuck and trap moisture, causing rot; and the tedious process of covering (and uncovering) the trees.

* Choose the fine-woven netting on the market that has recently revolutionized organic pest control. It is synthetic fabric sold as 'Vege Net', 'PlantGuard', 'Fruit Saver' or 'Veggie Saver'. This keeps out not only birds, but destructive insects as well, and is a valuable asset to fruit-growers.

* An electronic bird-scarer is perhaps the best alternative. These devices are motion-activated, and fall into three main types.

- The first is a sprinkler. When the bird moves within range of the motion sensor it triggers a 3-second burst of water in the direction of the bird. The noise and movement gets quick results!
- The second repeller works by playing sound recordings of real life predator birds. The device is triggered by the movement of the bird in front of the sensor. Results are impressive; birds flee in panic!
- The final type of electronic deterrent is the sonic alarm. When the detector senses the bird it triggers a burst of ultrasonic and/or audible sound. Some deterrents also include flashing lights. Any of these three bird-scarers will be highly effective in protecting your fruit from birds.

CODLING MOTH

The codling moth is a pest of European descent, the wormlike larvae of which feed on apples as well as pears, quinces, walnuts and stonefruits. The adult codling moth is around 10 mm long - gray-brown with a 20 mm wingspan and a shimmering metallic seeming copper patch on the wingtips. The larvae will be white or pink caterpillars, with a dark brown head.

Lifecycle

Codling moths appear in early spring, in blossom season. The female moth lays minuscule eggs, the size of pin-heads, on the leaves. These eggs hatch after ten days, and the small caterpillars feed on leaves before making their way to the fruit. The larva burrows into the core of the fruit, and feeds there for three to five weeks.

When it becomes time for the larva to pupate, the larva leaves the fruit, moving down the branches and trunk of the tree, seeking a safe place to cocoon - such as loose bark, crevices or somewhere on ground. After pupating, the adult moths emerge to repeat the cycle. This will take place two to three times a year, with a winter dormancy period.

Signs of Infestation

Codling moth larvae will ruin the fruit they infest, and making them all but inedible to humans. Damaged fruit will usually fall prematurely. A large infestation can severely damage the tree's crop. In addition, the larva may also damage the leaves of the tree, causing defoliation.

Organic Control Methods

Fruit should be inspected every ten days. If small holes are found in the skin, this is a sign a codling moth has entered. Infested fruit must be plucked and destroyed - either fed to animals, burnt, submerged in water for several days or 'cooked' by leaving it in the sun while in a sealed black plastic bag.

Letting chickens roam under the trees will make sure fallen fruit is eaten (along with the larvae). Do not allow chickens to roam under young trees however, as their scratching may damage the roots.

Codling moth cocoons are often found under pieces of flaking bark or litter, especially if such detritus is let to collect in the crotch of the tree. Regularly check and clear the tree of such rubbish to remove hiding places for codling moth cocoons.
Ladders, boxes and tree props can also be shelters for cocoons - remove all such equipment from the orchard if they aren't being immediately used.

Encourage the codling moth's greatest natural enemy, the Trichogramma wasp, by planting flowers or herbs high in pollen and nectar around the base of the tree. Suitable plants include clover, alyssum, cosmos, coriander, mustard, dill and Queen Anne's Lace.

Make sure your garden is a safe place for other predators of the moth, including ants, earwigs, spiders, ichneumon wasps, chalcid wasps, carabid wasps - as well as night-flying birds, insectivorous bats and tree frogs.

Spread horticultural glue in a thick ring around the trunk of the tree to prevent the female moths from crawling up the tree to lay their eggs. Apply this glue at the first sighting of the moths, and leave it on the tree until midwinter.

Place corrugated cardboard bands around the trunk, above the horticultural glue. This will force larvae to crawl into the cardboard when they start to seek a place to pupate.

Codling moths can be baited using open mouthed jars filled with a solution of fermenting apple juice, molasses, oil of cloves or port mixed with water, which are then hung in the trees for two weeks at a time. Apply a thin layer of vegetable oil over the surface to prevent mosquitoes breeding, and to trap the moths. An effective light trap can be created by suspending a light bulb above a dish or pan of water, over the surface of which has been poured a layer of kerosene.

Overhead irrigation used from 7-11pm during the peak months of moth activity has been observed to increase larval mortality and reduce egg laying - reducing fruit damage by up to 90%.

If you have only a few trees, consider bagging your fruit, covering them with waxed paper or cloth. The bag should be removed four days before harvest. This not only protects the fruit from codling moth larvae and other boring insects, but from birds, fruit bats and possums also.

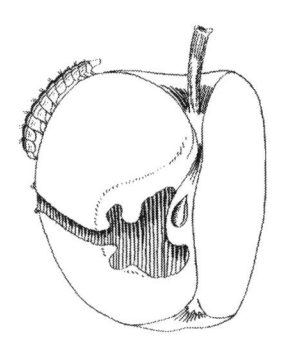

EARWIGS

Although earwigs can devastate maturing soft fruit, they also have a beneficial role and are important predators of aphids.

Earwigs feed most actively at night. During the day they hide in dark, cool, moist places - often beneath loose clods of soil, boards, or dense growth of vines or weeds or even within fruit damaged by other pests such as snails or birds. Earwigs love living in mulch, particularly sugarcane mulch. Swap sugar cane mulch around your strawberries to pine needle mulch.

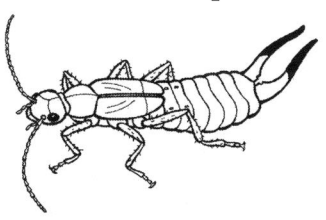

Signs of Infestation

Earwigs can dig lumps out of low-growing fruits such as strawberries. They can chew holes in ripening peaches and other stonefruit.

Organic control methods

These include trapping, natural predators, organic insecticides and sanitation. Use a combination of these for best effect.

Trapping

* Place numerous traps throughout your garden, hiding them near shrubbery, in garden beds and against fences.

* Putting some food bait in the trap can improve its efficiency. Wheat bran and wheat germ are effective baits. Dampening the bait may soften it and make it more inviting.

* You could alternatively pour 2 cm of fish oil (such as tuna oil) in the bottom of a low-sided can, such as a cat food or tuna fish can. Vegetable oil with a drop of bacon grease can also be used. Sink the can into the ground so that the top of the can is at soil level. Earwigs will be attracted to the fish oil during the night, when they feed. Keep the level of the oil at least 2 cm below the can's rim, forcing the earwigs to crawl deeply into the container. Many earwigs will simply fall in and drown. Every morning, get rid of the trapped earwigs and refill cans with fish oil.

* Other good types of traps are rolled-up newspapers, scrunched up newspaper, corrugated cardboard, or small tubes such as lengths of bamboo, short pieces of hose, pieces of old galvanised water pipe or the hollow metal tubing of old gates. Put these traps on the ground near the earwig-affected plants every evening just before dark.

* Alternatively, place halved orange or lemon skins upside down around the garden to trap earwigs.

* Earwig baits are often ineffective where other attractive food sources are nearby - such as your ripening strawberries! Sprinkle baits around susceptible plants before they become infested. Once earwigs have already invaded susceptible plants or fruit trees with ripening fruit, baits will probably fail to control the problem.

How to dispose of trapped earwigs
The earwigs in such traps should be collected every 2-3 days and tied up in a plastic bag before being discarded. In the mornings, shake the earwigs that have gathered in your traps into a pail of soapy water. Earwigs can also be dropped into a sturdy plastic bag and crushed. Continue this routine every day until your traps are are no longer catching earwigs.

Natural Predators
Chickens and ducks love to feast on earwigs. Other natural enemies include frogs, lizards and birds.

Chemical Control
Pythrethrum spray or Neem oil can be used against earwigs. Insecticides containing spinosad are the most effective, environmentally sound products.

Other more toxic insecticides are available, but they are usually detrimental to bees and other beneficial wildlife.

To get the best effect, apply them before the infestation is severe, following all instructions on the label and making sure the product is suitable for use your fruiting plants. To protect daytime bees, apply insecticides in the evening.

Sanitation
*Enhance your trapping program by getting rid of shelter sites for earwigs such as thick ground-cover plants, weeds, piles of rubbish and fallen leaves.

*Avoid growing dense ground cover plants such as ivy close to your strawberry patch. You might have to clear away or thin out your mulches, or replace them with pine needles.

*Make sure the bases of your fruit trees' trunks are free from weeds, grass and suckers all through the year. Any such foliage provides shelter for earwigs.

*Keep an eye on earwig populations by placing scrunched up or folded newspapers or hessian bags at the foot of trees and checking them for earwigs in the morning.

*Gently scrape off the loose bark from the lower trunks of older fruit trees. Trunks can be painted sticky, non-drying horticultural glues such as Trappit or Tanglefoot. This prevents earwigs from climbing up the trunks to reach ripening stonefruit.

* Keep your fruit trees pruned, thin out any heavy crops, and pick fruit as soon as it ripens. These procedures will help away earwigs.

* Earwigs can be very useful in fruit trees when they are feeding on aphids, so you don't really need to worry about them in trees that do not produce soft fruit.

EUROPEAN RED MITE

European red mites feed on the juices and chlorophyll within the leaves of pear, apple and stonefruit trees. Adult mites are dark red, with white spots on their backs. The immature mites (instars) are bright red (but may also be green if they are seen just after moulting).

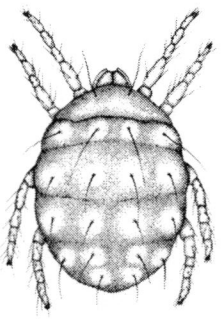

European red mites go through three instars before they fully mature. The adult female lays the globular red eggs (each of which sports a thin stalk or stipe rising from the top) on young leaves or, if laid in winter, at the bases of twig buds and spur. The eggs may also be laid in areas where the tree has suffered some damage.

Signs of Infestation

Leaf damage caused by the feeding of European red mites looks like a mottling on the surface of the leaves, accompanied by an overall lightening of color. If the infestation is large, leaf bronzing may occur, and in hot weather this can lead to mite burn (in which portions, or even the entirety of the leaf, turn brown and dry).

Organic Control Methods

* European red mite can be controlled by spraying the trees during the winter dormancy period.
* Biological balance can be restored through encouraging the red mite's natural predators - green and brown lacewings, pirate bugs and predatory mites.
* Mites thrive in dusty conditions - try to ensure your orchard is free from excess dust.
* Some pear strains are more tolerant of mites than others. Red pears are the least prone to damage.

FRUIT PIERCING MOTH

Fruit piercing moths feed on many host plants, including bananas, citruses, figs, stonefruit, mangoes and guavas. The adult insects are large (100mm wingspan) with plump bodies.

Their forewings may be green, brown or cream-colored, while the hindwings are yellow-orange with black patches.

Larvae are black and velvety, with a white spot on each side just in front of the first pair of prolegs.

Signs of Infestation

The adult moths feed by piercing ripe or ripening fruit and sucking the juice. At the site of the piercing, beneath the skin, the fruit will become bruised and dry. In addition, secondary pests or diseases may enter the fruit through the hole, causing even more extensive damage.

Fruit piercing moth

Organic Control Methods

- Protect ripening fruit by netting trees with fine-woven nets such as 'Fruit Saver', or bagging individual fruit during the early harvest period.
- Moth baits have been found to have some success in controlling this pest. See Home Made Pest Remedies.

FRUIT SPOTTING BUG

The fruit spotting bug (Amblypelta nitida or A. lutescens) is a Queensland native insect common to the Atherton Tableland and sometimes observed elsewhere in coastal and subcoastal Queensland.

This pest sucks the juices from the fruits of tropical and subtropical trees, including avocados as well as guavas, mangoes, lychees, bananas and macadamias.

During its lifecycle this insect will pass through multiple stages - from tiny 1.7mm semi-triangular green eggs (laid singly) that turn darker and more opalescent with time, to a series of five 'instars' (nymphs) before becoming adult.

Identifying a fruit-spotting bug in one of its nymphal stages can be complex, as each instar looks different. The first appears like a green and black ant, while the subsequent instars are either green or orange-brown. By the third instar the bug will have developed wing buds. Fortunately fruit-spotting nymphs can be identified by the black and noticeably flattened second-last segments on their antennae.

The adult fruit-spotter is a dark green-brown bug with large prominent antennae and scent glands on the upper abdomen (white-circled in A. lutescens), approximately 1.5cm long.

Although the fruit-spotting bug lays its eggs singly, a female may lay 150 eggs or more in its lifetime. After six or seven days, the nymph will emerge, and the journey to adulthood takes around six weeks. Adult fruit-spotters tend to congregate in orchard 'hot spots' (small groups of trees). An orchard may see three or four generations of fruit-spotters each year.

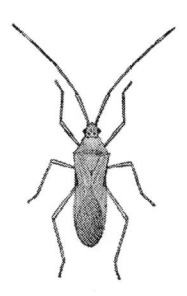

Fruit spotting bug

Signs of Infestation

Both the adults and immature nymph fruit-spotters feed on a fruit's juice after piercing the skin. During the feeding process they exude saliva from their mouthparts that act to break down plant cells, causing brown lesions to develop on the seeds and black 'pin-pricks' to emerge on the inside of the skin. spots to develop around the bites.

Fruit-spotting bugs can cause massive crop loss of green (unripe) fruit if a heavy infestation targets a tree. Mature fruit tend not to be as damaged.

Organic Control Methods

- To identify 'hot spots', examine and dissect green fallen fruits from beneath all trees.
- Encourage natural predators such as egg parasitoids, assassin bugs and spiders, to target these large beetles
- Organic and non-toxic sprays (such as those described Commercial and Home Made Pest Remedies) can be useful control tools. Reapply every 2-3 weeks.
- Given that the fruit-spotting bug is an Australian native species, avoid planting orchards in close proximity to bushland.

GRASSHOPPERS

Grasshoppers prefer to live in grassland, but as the grasses dry out in summer, and food becomes scarce, they often move into other areas in search of fresh, green food. They can make their way into gardens and orchards, feeding on cherry, apple, pear, citrus and stonefruit trees along with other fruit crops. Large swarms of grasshoppers are devastating to fruit trees.

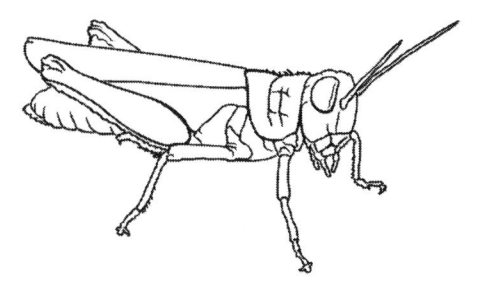

Signs of Infestation

The damage from grasshopper feeding shows up as big holes or cutouts along leaf margins, missing leaves and flowers, and big green insects hopping about. Grasshoppers usually chew on soft plant tissue, such as leaves and flowers, rather than fruit. However in large numbers they can devastate entire trees or even orchards.

Organic Control Methods

Biological Controls of Grasshoppers

Birds (such as swamp ibis, guinea fowl and chickens) are grasshoppers' primary natural enemies. Chickens especially can be a great addition to a garden, if they are properly contained in a chicken run or are let run loose under well established fruit trees. Other grasshopper predators include reptiles (lizards and snakes), predatory and parasitic insects (such as assassin bugs, ants, tachnid or robber flies and parasitic wasps) and sugar gliders.

These beneficial predators can be encouraged by establishing plenty of nectar-producing plants such as clover, coriander, dill and Sweet Alice (Alyssum).

Physical and Cultural Controls of Grasshoppers

It is easier to catch grasshoppers in the early morning when they are sluggish. They can be caught by hand or with a butterfly net. Mosquito netting or floating row covers can be used to protect garden beds in the early part of the season.

Grasshoppers are said to be attracted to the color yellow - this can be exploited to trap them in a variety of ways. Floating yellow plastic on ponds or paddling pools can lure grasshoppers to a watery grave. Similarly yellow sticking tape can be used as a trap.

Grasshoppers are attracted to canola oil, and will be lured to a variety of traps, such as molasses traps or water traps. Chilli sprays can also be effective. For more information, see the chapter Homemade Pest Remedies.

LIGHT BROWN APPLE MOTH

The larva of the light brown apple moth feeds on the leaves of pome fruit (such as pears and apples) as well as some stonefruit (such as apricots). The moth is native to Australia, where its natural predators generally keep the population in check.

The adult moths are buff colored, around 10 mm long, but they are rarely seen. The larvae begin their lives as tiny yellow caterpillars, 1 mm long. To protect themselves, they spin a web on the underside of the leaf, under which they feed in relative safety. After moulting, the larger caterpillar constructs a nest made from leaves and or fruit, webbed together. As time passes the caterpillar grows, until they reach 25 mm in length, brown-headed with a pale green body, and striped down the center with a darker green stripe.

Light brown apple moth larvae are present from blossom to harvest. Although the larvae themselves may be sometimes difficult to spot, the webbing they create is easier to see - in blossom clusters and under leaves, usually within the lower half or central branches of the tree.

Signs of Infestation

Light brown apple moth do not tend to severely damage trees - causing some damage to webbed leaves and superficial damage to fruit when webbing is created between a cluster of fruit. It is uncommon for the larvae to enter the fruit, but it does happen occasionally that a larva will enter through the calyx or stem area and feed.

Organic Control Methods

Organic insecticides can be used, including Dipel, EcoGrub, Insect Hotel, Success and pyrethrum products.

The most important controls of the light brown apple moth are biological - natural parasitoid predators such as the tachinid fly, the braconid wasp and the ichneumonid wasp.

MEALYBUGS

Mealybugs are common pests which attack a range of host plants - from passionfruit and cashews to cassava, citruses, mangoes and many others. They are small insects which suck the tree's phloem sap. Adult females and nymphs (soft, white, wax-covered and sporting long tail filaments) are more commonly seen than the tiny, winged males.

Lifecycle
Most mealybugs start their life as eggs, however some species such as the female long-tailed mealybug lay no eggs, instead giving birth to two live nymphs. All mealybugs go through a 'crawler' stage, before becoming wax-covered adults. In a garden infested with mealybugs, you will likely observe two to four generations of these pests per year, regardless of season.

Signs of Infestation

The phloem sap upon which the mealybug feeds carries vital nutrients to the tree. As a result, a large infestation of mealybugs can significantly reduce the vigour of the tree. Other symptoms include yellowing of leaves, defoliation and fruit-drop. Since the mealybug secretes a sticky sweet honeydew, they are often also accompanied by sooty mold, which fouls the leaves, fruit and branches, sometimes blocking photosynthesis. Depending on the species of mealybug, other forms of damage might occur, such as plant deformation in cassavas, and virus transmission in pineapples.

Organic Control Methods

Fortunately mealybugs have many natural predators, which keep them under control. These include the larvae of green lacewings and predatory flies, ladybeetles and parasitic wasps - insects which can be encouraged by planting flowers high in pollen and nectar near the trees.

Be always on the alert for mealybug infestations - check new growths and the joints and undersides of leaves regularly for crawlers.

Weak, stressed plants are most susceptible to mealybugs. Therefore maintaining healthy plants is a useful defensive strategy. Individual mealybugs can be rubbed away or picked off. Mealybugs can be washed away by directing a steady stream of water onto them, such as from a hose. A light infestation can be quite easily managed in this way.

Spray the affected areas of the plant with a solution of insecticidal soap or neem oil. The latter has a double benefit, acting as a fungicide. Make sure the spray comes in contact with the bugs.

An all-purpose kitchen insecticidal spray can be made from steeping a mixture onion, garlic and cayenne pepper for an hour, before straining and adding a tablespoon of liquid dishwashing soap.

MIRID BUG

Mirid bugs ,or 'tea mosquitoes' (Helopeltis sp.) are common pests in northern Queensland which feed on many fruiting trees and vines - including cashews, avocados, cocoa, mangoes, guava and passionfruit.

Adult mirid bugs are red-brown insects with orange thoraxes, and long fragile legs. They are 6.5-8.5mm in length. Their eggs are only a millimetre long - white and elongated - laid singly or in clusters on young leaves' stems and petioles.

After a week the first instar emerges - the first of five iterations. Instar nymphs look similar to adult mirids, although they are lighter orange-brown and have no wings.

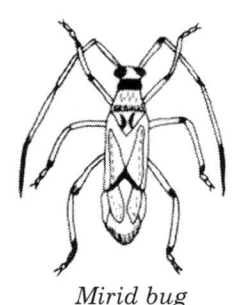

Mirid bug

They feed on leaves and shoots until, 10-16 days after hatching, they become adult, and live for several weeks more, mating and sucking the juices from leaves and shoots. Female adults will often lay between 30 and 50 eggs.

Signs of Infestation

The feeding habits of the mirid bug lead to the formation of distorting lesions along the veins of young leaves, bunched terminal growth and brown sunken spots on fruit. This is similar to the damage of the fruit-spotting bug.

Organic Control Methods

Check trees regularly for the presence of mirid bugs. If bugs are found, spray immediately with an appropriate organic pesticide.

Green tree ants can, if properly managed, serve as effective biological controls for mirid bugs. However care should be taken to not let their population get out of control, as they have a symbiotic relationship with other garden pests like scale and mealybug.

PEAR AND CHERRY SLUG

Pear and Cherry Slugs are small black slug-like grubs of the glossy black sawfly (Caliroa cerasi), which are laid as eggs on the leaves of trees and shrubs belonging to the fruit family Rosaceae (e.g. plums, pears, apples, cherries and quinces).

After hatching, the grubs feed voraciously, stripping leaves to skeletons before dropping to the ground and pupating to create a new generation of adults that will cause another wave of tiny grubs to strip the tree.

There are two generations of grubs a year – the first emerging in spring and the second in summer. The second generation is worse than the first, and if left unchecked, will completely skeletonise a tree's leaves, weakening or even killing it. Pear and cherry slugs particularly enjoy humid weather.

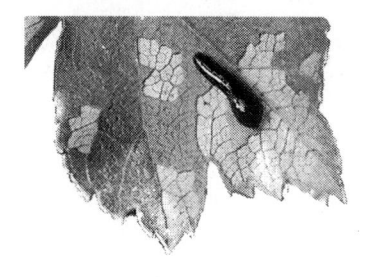

Signs of Infestation

The first signs of pear and cherry slug are little brown dead patches in the green of the leaves, which spread until the leaves look 'lacy'. The grubs themselves are translucent and slimy brown-black, with a bulbous shape at the head.

Organic Control Methods

- Throwing wood ash, chalk or flour over the infested tree desiccates the grubs' skin, killing them. Wood ash (from a log fire) has a beneficial side effect, adding potash to the soil, which acts as a fertilizer.
- First-generation pear and cherry slugs can be picked and squished by hand (although this is a rather distasteful job).
- Alternatively they can be hosed off with a gentle jet of water.
- Spraying the trees with lime first in spring and again in midsummer is an effective control-measure, however the use of too much lime is to be avoided since it changes the pH of the soil underneath the tree.
- Bacillus thuringiensis (BT) is a biological control that can be sprayed on the tree to naturally control the pear and cherry grubs.
- Long term control involves encouraging natural predatory insects (such as lacewings and hoverflies), spiders and birds to flourish in the garden, by planting flowering shrubs near the trees.
- Letting chickens roam around under the trees in the winter can also help keep the soil clear of sawfly wasp pupae, meaning that they don't come out in spring to lay their eggs.

PHYTOPHTHORA

Phytophthora (or 'water-molds') are potentially devastating plant parasites. Although they share many similarities to fungi - both in effect and appearance, they are in fact belong to a different kingdom, the Chromalveolata. They can affect many different plant hosts - including apples, avocados, almonds, stonefruit, oaks and vegetables. Phytophthora can infect roots, crown, graft area and branches and is potentially devastating to a crop.

Signs of Infection

One of the first signs of phytophthora is a plant that fails to thrive, despite regular watering and the appropriate application of fertilizer. This is a sign of damaged roots. As the disease progresses, crown rot, cankers on the trunks, branch dieback and fruit rot may occur.

Organic Control Methods

Although phytophthora is not a true fungus, it responds to fungicide treatment.

The disease can be quite easily prevented, as the organism requires a prolonged period of standing water (around the roots, crown of the tree or crotch between branches). Avoiding this goes a long way to preventing infection - when planning an orchard, do not plant in waterlogged areas.

Arrange your irrigation system and set timers so as not to overwater any areas.

If you have established trees, focus on keeping the soil healthy since it will prevent the growth of phytophthora and promote a vigorous, infection-resistant tree.

Organic soil amendments such as animal manure, urea and compost will help fertilize the tree and improve the soil structure. The decomposing matter releases ammonia and volatile organic acids which kill phytophthora. These amendments also encourage the growth of biological control organisms in the soil which help to keep phytopthora populations down.

Mulching is recommended, as it facilitates drainage. Certain types of mulch inhibit the growth of phytophthora - these include alfalfa meal, wheat straw, cotton waste and soybean meal.

If buying plants from a nursery, check to see if the plants have been standing on plastic sheeting where standing water may have collected. Look at the roots to see if they are brown and soft - a sign of phytophthora.

POSSUMS

Possums are one of the few animals that have adapted to urban environments as the human race swiftly infiltrates and dominates their ancestral lands, destroying the native habitat these harmless creatures have enjoyed for millennia.

They are graceful, agile animals who are simply trying to survive. When we bulldoze their traditional food sources and plant our fruit trees, they turn to those trees for nourishment. This - of course - leads to a conflict of interests between possums and gardeners.

From the RSPCA's website: 'Brushtail (Trichosurus vulpecula) and Ringtail (Pseudocheirus peregrinus) possums are native marsupial species that have adapted well to urbanisation and are commonly found dwelling in Australian gardens.

Ringtail possums are a social species that live in nests, called dreys, several metres above the ground. They build them out of bark and leaves and usually dwell in them as a family. Brushtail possums are larger, more territorial possums that usually reside in tree hollows. The trees and gardens around our houses provide a modified woodland environment similar to their natural habitat and both species feed on native plants found in abundance in suburban gardens.'

Signs of Possums

Signs that possums are foraging in your garden include fruit missing from trees, upper leaves chewed, citrus fruit skinned, blossom buds and flowers eaten.

Organic Control Methods

To keep possums from raiding your fruit, try these techniques:

Netting: use tight-stretched netting to protect your trees. Loose netting is very dangerous for wild birds and animals, as they can easily become entangled in it, which is highly distressing for gardeners, and usually lethal to the animal.
One method of netting a single tree involves planting four tall star pickets around the tree in late summer or early autumn, just before the fruit is ripe.

Take two long sections of flexible plastic pipe or hose, bend them into a u-shape and push the end of each hose down over the star pickets so that they form two round arches at right angles to each other, crossing in the middle, directly above the tree. You now have a dome-shaped frame made of two crossing arches.

Throw your netting over this frame, allowing it to drape down and touch the ground all the way around. Tighten the netting as much as possible and anchor the hem to the ground with u-pins or bricks. Remove the netting after harvesting the fruit.

Banding tree trunks: Possums cannot climb up tree trunks when a wide, slippery band obstructs their path. Tree bands are commercially available. They are often used in public parks and gardens where trees are widely spaced apart and possums have to run along the ground to reach the next tree.

Interrupting possums' 'aerial roads': When trees are growing close together, possums do not have to descend to the ground. When foraging for food, they simply jump from branch to branch or run along wires, fence tops or roofs to reach their destination.

Interrupt these aerial roads by pruning back trees, or mounting plastic spikes on fence tops. The spikes do not hurt the animals, but they make it impossible for them to pass.

Motion activated water blasts: (see 'birds').

Ultra sonic deterrents: These devices emit a high-pitched sound that is supposed to be inaudible by humans. The sound repels possums (as well as other outdoor pests such as cats, foxes, rabbits and bats) - a humane and effective deterrent. Be aware, however, that many humans can hear the sound and it has the same annoying effect on them.

Possums can be encouraged to avoid fruit trees and ornamental plants by sprinkling blood and bone fertilizer (the smell of which is distasteful to the possums) around the base of the tree.

Deterrent Sprays: Spraying trees with a garlic and chilli solution: Take several cloves of garlic and a handful of hot chillies. Wearing rubber gloves, chop the vegetables finely and place in a large pot, just covered with water. Bring to the boil then turn off the heat. Allow to stand overnight, then strain.

Pour this mixture into a sprayer and liberally douse your fruit trees with it. If it rains, you will have to repeat the process. Possums don't like the smell of garlic, and the chilli is a good deterrent too!

A simple spray can be made with using the contents of the kitchen cupboard - English mustard mixed with detergent and diluted.

Tabasco sauce has also been found to be effective as a deterrent - dab it unadulterated onto the tree foliage or fruit. Any hungry possum will think twice before taking a second bite!

Another deterrent spray can be made by heating 100g of quassia chips in two litres of water for an hour, straining the liquid and adding a tablespoon of detergent. This liquid should be kept and diluted at a rate of 1:4 parts water before sprayed onto the plants.

A surprising deterrent spray is simply tea! Add four teaspoons of Lapsang Souchong tea to two litres of boiling water. Once the tea has been strained and cooled, it may be sprayed directly onto your plants.
The tea remedy lasts for two weeks before it should be reapplied with a fresh brew of tea. Make sure you spray after rain.

Sprays should be re-applied on a regular and ongoing basis - after rain, and every two or three weeks. These deterrents can also be sprayed on the 'highways' used by the possum, as well as on the fruit and foliage you want to protect. Encountering an unpleasant spicy substance on a well used route can upset the possum, disrupting their habit and encouraging them to seek food elsewhere. Breaking possum habits is a slow process however, so have patience and persist with the spraying.

Some commercial possum deterrents take the form of odor-emitters like Poss-Off or Scat.

Note: no one possum-control solution is guaranteed so ideally several of these methods should be practiced at once.

QUEENSLAND FRUIT FLY

There are more than 200 species of fruit fly native to Australia. Only a few of them cause problems for fruit growers, but those problems can be very serious.

The Queensland Fruit Fly (Bactrocera tryoni) strikes along the east coast of Australia; it is a native of its rainforest habitat. It attacks many varieties of fruit (and vegetables); notably pome fruit, stonefruit, figs, loquats, guavas, mangoes, feijoas and citrus. As well as decreasing fruit production and making fruit inedible, this pest seriously affects local and international trade.
In southern areas where winters are long and cold, fruit fly die off, making control simpler to achieve. This pest is generally not a problem in Victoria and Tasmania; however in 2008, for the first time in twenty years, there was an outbreak of Queensland
When the larvae are fully grown they crawl out of the fruit and burrow into the ground, where they pupate, preparing to become flies.

The fruit fly population reaches a peak in late summer.

Please contact the Department of Primary Industries on 136 186 (Victoria only) if you suspect any of your plants have fruit fly.

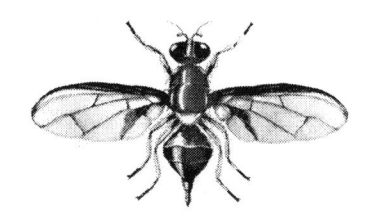

Signs of Infestation

You can tell if fruit has been attacked by the fly, for the skin will appear dimpled, or will weep drops of a clear liquid. Eventually the fruit will rot and drop.

If you're finding brown spots dotted all throughout the flesh of your citrus fruit, this is a sign of a secondary bacterial infection that follows fruit fly stinging the fruit. Even if the maggots haven't developed, the bacteria still enters and causes these brown rotting spots.

Organic Control Methods

Natural predators: Do all you can to increase habitats for the fruit fly's natural predators, which include birds, ground beetles, spiders and ants. Encourage poultry to forage beneath your fruit trees.

Sanitation: Collect fallen infected fruit as soon as it drops, before larvae have a chance to leave from the fruit and burrow into the soil to pupate. It is essential that you destroy this fruit, so as to break the cycle.

To kill the larvae, place fruit in a black plastic bag, seal the bag and place it in full sun to 'cook'. Alternatively, submerge infected fruit in a sealed bucket of water and leave it for a few days. You could also immerse the fruit in a pot of water and bring it to the boil, then use the cooked fruit as a food source for poultry.

Longan - fruit fly resistant fruit

Traps: Queensland Fruit Fly is a species that responds well to the careful placement of baits and traps. The aim here is to attract and trap as many female fruit flies as possible before they have the chance to lay their eggs. Pheromones work well as bait to trap the male fly before it has an opportunity to play its part in reproduction.

Many types of fruit fly traps and lures are commercially available - or you can make your own.

<u>Make your own fruit fly traps</u>
You will need a plastic drink bottle, a drill and some string or wire. Drill a few holes, about 10 millimetres wide, spaced out evenly, about half-way up the bottle. These are the holes through which the fruit flies will enter, attracted by the bait inside. (Making the holes is a lot easier if you choose a bottle with a square cross-section rather than a round bottle that may roll about while you are drilling.) If you don't have a drill, you can make the holes with a heated metal skewer.

Home made fruit fly trap

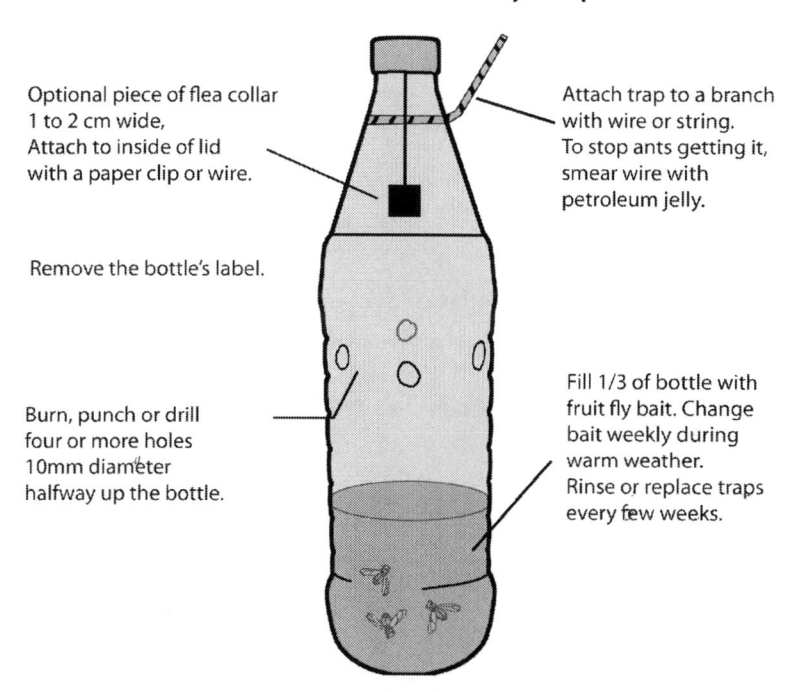

Optional piece of flea collar 1 to 2 cm wide, Attach to inside of lid with a paper clip or wire.

Remove the bottle's label.

Burn, punch or drill four or more holes 10mm diameter halfway up the bottle.

Attach trap to a branch with wire or string. To stop ants getting it, smear wire with petroleum jelly.

Fill 1/3 of bottle with fruit fly bait. Change bait weekly during warm weather. Rinse or replace traps every few weeks.

Pour some bait into the bottom of the bottle. For the bait you can simply use fruit juice; however, to make a bait that's irresistible to fruit flies, add to the juic a pinch of sugar and a dash of brewers' yeast. The yeast and sugar will ferment, making a sweet brew.

For extra potency use a length of wire to suspend a 2cm strip of pet flea collar from the lid inside the container.
Tie a string or wire around the neck of the lure-filled bottle and hang two or three of these home made traps in every fruit tree. During fruit fly season, change the lure once a week, as the bottle will fill up with dead fruit flies and possibly other insects.
Fruit exclusion: 'Fruit exclusion' is probably the most effective

organic fruit fly solution for home fruit-growers. Covering all individual fruits or the whole tree with insect exclusion netting, cloth or paper can prevent fruit fly infestation.

Garden shops and nurseries sell bags of various sizes, suitable for the size and shape of the fruit you want to protect. Most of these bags are re-usable. An added advantage of this method is that bags also protect fruit from birds and sunburn.

Fruit tree selection: If possible, select trees that bear fruit early in the season, thus missing the fruit fly population explosion. Growing dwarf trees, or keeping trees pruned to manageable size (under 2.5 m high) may also help. With smaller trees it is easier to practise fruit fly control methods such as exclusion. Furthermore, smaller crop yields are more manageable and having small trees helps avoid potential sources of fruit fly infestations from unharvested fruit remaining on tree branches too high to reach easily.

Fruit fly resistant fruits include:

- Avocado (avoid thin-skinned Fuerte and Rincon)
- Bananas
- Blueberry (sometimes affected)
- Citrus (avoid thin-skinned varieties such as Meyer lemon)
- Custard Apple (winter ripening varieties are best)
- Grapes (sometimes affected)
- Grumichama
- Ice Cream Bean
- Jaboticaba
- Kiwifruit
- Longan and Lychee
- Macadamia
- Mulberry (sometimes affected)

- Nashi Pears (sometimes affected)
- Passionfruit
- Pawpaw
- Persimmon (early varieties like Fuyu are susceptible)
- Pineapples
- Pomegranate

Information source: Green Harvest

RABBITS

Rabbits, while cute, can severely damage your garden, since they feed on a very wide range of common garden plants, including trees, shrubs, vegetables, fruits and herbaceous plants. New growth and young plants are particularly favoured, but rabbits will also eat mature foliage and even bark.

Signs of Infestation

Evening and early morning are the best times to catch rabbits feeding in the garden, since most of their grazing takes place under cover of darkness. Their spherical droppings are also easily identifiable signs of their having taken up residence.

Spiral rabbit-proof tree guard

Rabbit damage can include:

- Shoots on herbaceous plants grazed to ground level.
- Foliage and soft shoots of woody plants can be grazed up to a height of 50cm (20in) by rabbits standing up on their hind legs.
- Bark may be gnawed away from the base of trunks, especially in winter when snow or frost makes other vegetation unavailable. This can kill trees and shrubs if ringbarked.
- Rabbits also dig holes and scrapes in lawns and flower beds.

Organic Control Methods

Fences: Rabbit-proof fences and gates help prevent these furry pests from entering your garden from your neighbours' properties, farms or surrounding bushland. An ideal fence is 1.4m high, constructed from 2.5cm wire mesh, with 30cm of the wire sunk underground. The lower 15cm of the underground portion should be bent outwards, to prevent rabbits from burrowing underneath.

Wire netting: If the thought of fortifying your entire property with rabbit-proof fencing is too daunting (or too much effort), protect smaller at-risk areas (such as kitchen gardens) with wire netting. Individual plants can be given the same treatment.

Tree guards: Use plastic tree guards to protect the trunks of your trees from bark-stripping rabbits. If the bark has been already damaged, wrap the partially-gnawed trunk in black polythene to encourage the damaged area to callus over.

Sprays: Some protection can be afforded by the use of an animal-repelling spray. Not all are suitable for use on edible fruit near to harvest time however. For these and other edible plants, avoid sprays containing aluminium ammonium sulphate. Bear in mind that even the best sprays are best used in conjunction with other animal-deterrents, since they rarely provide complete protection.

RATS

Signs of Infestation

If you notice that your fruit disappears mysteriously the day before it was ripe enough to pick, or the rind is chewed off your citrus fruits, or the gnawed remains of fruit is lying under your trees, then you are probably the victim of rat thieves Rats are smaller, cleverer, lighter and quieter than possums. When darkness falls they can shin up a twig, break off a small fruit with their paws and carry it back to the nest - all in the twinkling of an eye.

Rats will eat almost anything organic. Fruits they are partial to include citrus fruits, figs, pomegranates, stonefruit, nuts, apples, pears and guavas. They will eat the equivalent of around 10 percent of their body weight each day.

Nocturnal by nature, rats are most active during darkness. The visible presence of rats in the daytime may signify several things - that the rat is seeking food, that something (like a predator) has disturbed the rat's nest; or that your rat infestation is pretty serious.

Organic Control Methods

Even rats and mice deserve humane treatment. Poisons and sticky traps are cruel, but there are other ways to deter these pests.

Sprays: If your rat problem is localised to specific areas of the garden, a natural deterrent spray like tea-tree oil, naphthalene, chilli-oil or (PETA's preferred mixture) a mixture of horseradish, garlic and cayenne pepper can help keep the rats away.

Traps: If rat populations have exploded to the point that they are seriously damaging or causing disease, it may become necessary to resort to humane methods of killing. A spring trap is the most efficient, painless and eco-friendly trapping option. For your own sake, choose one with a metal or plastic base (for easy cleaning) and wear gloves and a dust mask when you dispose of the bodies. Do check your traps regularly, because occasionally an animal may be only wounded by one, and you don't want it to suffer.

Natural predators: If you live in a poison-free neighbourhood you can use a cat or a rat terrier to keep the rodent population under control. Rat terriers are particularly quick at dispatching their prey, and the rodent usually dies instantly, giving it a humane death (and providing your pet with a sustainable meal).

Live traps: If you can't bear the thought of killing the rat, you can use a live trap to capture the animal and release it somewhere else. However according to PETA (People for the Ethical Treatment of Animals), for this to be a humane solution you must release the rat within 100m from where you caught it. This can cause problems unless you have some way of preventing the rat from returning.

ROOT KNOT NEMATODES

Nematodes, also known as 'eel worms' are colorless, worm-like creatures so small that they are invisible to the naked eye. They live in organically rich soil, and there are more than 20,000 species. Most of these do no damage to plants and some are even beneficial to plants. The root-knot nematodes, however, which are most numerous in summer, are plant parasites.

Many fruiting plants are vulnerable to root knot nematodes, but these pests usually causes most damage to strawberries, melons, peaches, bananas, grapes, passionfruit, pineapples and pawpaw.

Signs of Infestation

It is not easy to recognize when your plants are being attacked by nematodes. They are not obvious, like leaf-chewing pests, because they live underground. The young eat their way inside the plant's roots, where their destructive activities stimulate the growth of lumpy tumours. These nodules impede plants' ability to absorb nutrients and moisture. Deprived of sustenance, plants become weak and stunted, unable to produce much fruit, and susceptible to disease and infection.

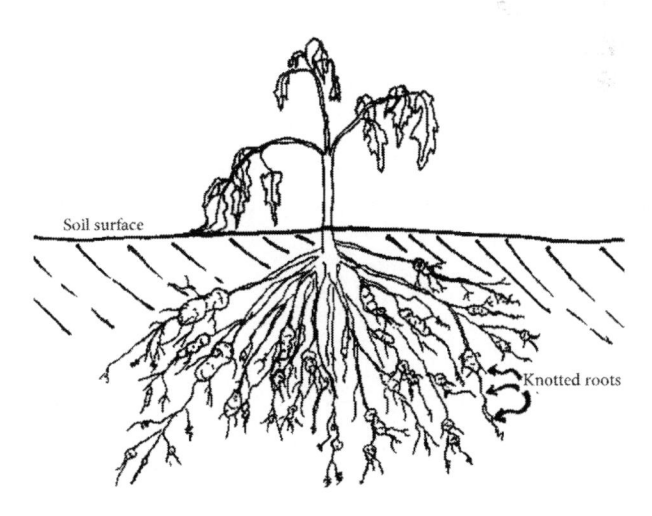

Signs of nematode attack include plants yellowing and wilting, and sometimes even dying. Plants may look as if they are suffering from drought, even when they are getting plenty of water. During the cooler months these symptoms may not be so obvious, but by summer when the numbers of nematodes increase, it may be too late to save your plants.

If you suspect that nematodes are infecting your plants, dig up one of the plants and rinse the soil off its roots. Inspect the roots for signs of lumps. These lumps may be tiny or huge, and they may affect only some of the roots or the entire root mass.
Keep in mind that healthy legumes such as beans and peas normally have lumps on their roots, because they absorb nitrogen from the atmosphere and fix it in the soil. So it's best not to use legumes for diagnosing nematodes!

Organic Control Methods

Natural predators: Encourage the proliferation of beneficial nematode species that prey on root knot nematodes. Harmless to humans, animals, plants, and healthy earthworms, beneficial nematodes are microscopic parasites that prey on the grubs and larvae of destructive insect pests such as weevils, chafers, borers, cut worms, termites, flies, ants, fleas and root knot nematodes. They kill their insect hosts within 48 hours.

To welcome them into your garden or orchard, create a rich organic environment for them by adding compost, manures and mulches to your soil.

Crop rotation: It's not really feasible to practice crop rotation with fruit trees or vines, but if you are growing strawberries, melons, bananas or pineapples, don't plant the same crops in the same soil every season. Move your crops around to make it harder for soil-dwelling root-knot nematodes to find them.

Sanitation: It's important to avoid throwing root knot nematode-infested roots into your compost heap! Instead, place them in a heavy duty plastic bag, seal up the bag and put it in the rubbish bin.

Natural soil biofumigants: After you have removed all plants from the soil that is affected by root-knot nematodes, broadcast mustard seeds across the entire area; in particular the mustard cultivar 'Nemagard'. Rake in the seeds, water them and let them grow. When the mustard plants are about 45 centimetres high, simply take a spade or mini-tiller and turn over the soil to 'dig in' the young mustard plants. Make sure the soil is moist - you may have to sprinkle it with some water.
Under the moist soil the green plant matter will start to decompose, giving off chemicals called 'isothiocyanates'. These compounds, which are what puts the heat into mustard, will naturally fumigate the soil, killing off many root-knot nematodes.

Do marigolds help?

Once a plant is infected by nematodes, there are not many options for treatment. As a result, most nematode management tactics are employed prior to planting the fruit crop.

Some gardeners plant cover crops to reduce nematode populations. A cover crop is a crop grown before the main crop is planted. In general, cover crops may be used as green manure, ploughed in to enrich the soil; or to control a pest that is unable to live on the cover crop, or to release certain organic compounds into the soil. Marigolds (Tagetes spp.) fall into the latter category.
Marigolds are best known for their ability to suppress plant-parasitic nematodes, but they can also be help protect plants against a variety of other pests.

Plants which release substances that can suppress other organisms are called 'allelopathic' plants. Marigolds are allelopathic; their living roots produce a substance called alpha-terthienyl, which can help reduce root-knot nematodes and other disease-causing organisms, such as fungi, bacteria, insects and viruses.

Not all marigold cultivars are 'resistant' host plants, able to suppress nematodes. Some have no effect on these pests at all (intermediate host plants), and others - which are called 'susceptible' host plants - can actually cause their numbers to increase. Different species of nematodes and the temperature of the soil also play a part in whether marigolds can be successful organic shields for your fruiting plants.

Marigolds

Meloidogyne incognita is a common and widely distributed species of root-knot nematode, but other species of root-knot nematodes are being discovered, which may be able to infect marigold cultivars which are resistant to other root-knot nematode species.

Marigolds may be resistant to some nematode species but may be very susceptible to others. How well marigolds perform is dependent on the marigold species and cultivar, and the species of nematode. Marigold cultivars that are 'resistant' to a particular nematode species may be used as cover crops to suppress that particular nematode.

African (Tagates erecta) and French (Tagates patula) marigolds have the best nematode controlling properties. They each have varieties that differ in flower size, shape, and color, in addition to plant size and leaf shape.

French and African marigolds can suppress 14 genera of plant-parasitic nematodes. They are most effective against lesion nematodes (Pratylenchus spp.), root-knot nematodes (Meloidogyne spp.) and possibly reniform nematodes. It should be noted that marigold may actually boost other nematode species, such as sting, stubby-root, spiral and awl nematodes.

French marigold cultivars appear to be most effective against the widest range of nematodes.

'Marigolds cannot eradicate nematodes. In order for marigold to have a continuous effect on nematode populations it must be grown every season before the actual crop is planted (Doubrava and Blake, 1999), because nematode populations will increase over time in the presence of susceptible crops like most vegetables and bedding plants.' *(McSorley et al., 1999)*.

'To really get the best out of marigolds, plant seedlings no less than 17 cm (7 inches) apart. Weeds can host nematodes, which ruins the effect of the marigolds; however dense planting helps stop weeds from sprouting. If you are sowing marigold seeds it is harder to ensure this regular spacing, so make sure you sprinkle plenty of seed on the soil to get thick coverage.'

(Quoted from *Marigolds (Tagetes spp.) for Nematode Management. R. Krueger, K. E. Dover, R. McSorley, K. H. Wan.*)

Research indicates that it is not useful to 'intercrop' marigold with other crops; ie, plant borders of marigolds, or rows of marigolds between rows of fruiting plants. It has been observed that this method fails to decrease plant-parasitic nematodes.

'Powers et al. (1993) showed that marigold intercropped with cucurbit was less productive than cucurbit monoculture and no effect on plant-parasitic nematodes was observed. On the other hand, El-Hamawi et al. (2004) showed that marigold used as an intercrop was effective in reducing M. incognita (Southern root-knot nematode). However, it should be pointed out that this experiment was conducted in pots, where root-knot severity might have been reduced because of soil dilution and a decreased density of host plants available for nematode reproduction.'

Quoted from *Marigolds (Tagetes spp.) for Nematode Management. R. Krueger, K. E. Dover, R. McSorley, K. -H. Wang*

Some people have tried inoculating soil with extracts of marigold, to control nematodes. This is of no benefit, however, because the nematicidal compound (alpha-tertheinyl) is only given off by healthy marigold roots living beneath the ground. As soon as the compound is exposed to sunlight it is deactivated.

For marigolds to best suppress plant-parasitic nematodes, you should use the following method:
- Determine which species of nematodes are living in your soil, if any.
- Next, choose the right species and cultivars of marigolds to control that nematode type.
- Plant the marigolds a minimum of nine weeks before your susceptible fruiting plants go into the ground.
- After the time has elapsed pull out the marigolds or dig them into the soil.
- Then position your fruiting crop in precisely the same spot

as the marigolds.
The soil will then be relatively free of nematodes at the time you plant your crop, but if these parasites creep back to infect your plants at a later date, planting marigolds among them will not 'cure' them.

Once root knot nematodes have infected your garden you can never be completely rid of them; however by keeping watch for signs of nematode damage and by using the techniques outlined above, you can certainly control them and keep your fruiting plants healthy.

Reference: Marigolds (Tagetes spp.) for Nematode Management R. Krueger, K. E. Dover, R. McSorley, K. -H. Wang.

RUST

Rust is an easily recognizable and common fungal disease that affects a wide range of hosts, including apples, stonefruit, pears, almonds and avocados. The disease has many varieties, each of which have similar effects and which are quite host specific.
Although rust will usually not kill the plant it infects, as the fungus requires a living host to survive and spread, it can stunt growth and cause widespread defoliation and crop loss.

Signs of Infection

The first sign of rust is the presence of yellow or brown spots on upper surfaces of leaves. The underside of the leaf will develop brown-orange pustules which are filled with powdery spores.

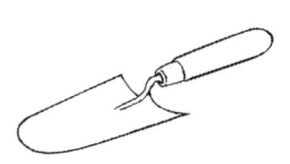

Organic Control Methods

It can be extremely difficult to completely eradicate rust once it has infected a plant.

Administer a seaweed extract fertilizer. The sulfur, potassium and trace elements (such as copper) contained in seaweed extract help strengthen the plant's cell walls and help prevent the spread of infection. Sulfur and copper fungicides can also be used, however bear in mind that these strong chemicals can harm beneficial predators.

If the infection is only mild, remove damaged leaves and burn or dispose of them in the rubbish bin sealed in a plastic bag.

SCALE AND SOOTY MOLD

Scales are small insects with rounded shells. They are related to whitefly, aphids and mealy bugs, and live by sucking the juices from leaves, usually positioning themselves along plant stems and the veins of leaves. Despite their tininess, they can cause severe damage to fruit trees.

There are many different varieties of scale, such as black scale, cottony-cushion scale, soft brown scale, white louse scale, pink wax scale, San Jose scale and red scale.

In their immature form, scale take the form of minuscule 'crawlers' that are windblown, or are carried by ants or birds to different plants. Mature scale are immobile, and many secrete a sticky sweet substance called honeydew, which often attracts ants. The ants 'farm' the scale for honeydew and protect from other predatory insects.

Sooty molds are fungi which cover plant leaves, stems and twigs with a black, powdery, sticky substance. In general these fungi feed off the honeydew secreted by the scale so where you see sooty mold you will probably also find scale, and vice versa. Sooty mold does not suck nourishment from plants, but because it covers leaf surfaces, it blocks out sunlight and decreases photosynthesis, thus stunting the plant's growth.

Getting rid of scale removes the source of the honeydew, which in turn kills off the sooty mold, which will eventually fall or wash off the foliage.

Signs of Infestation

Scale insects resemble small, dark bumps attached to leaves and stems. It is easy to overlook them, because they are so small, and because they generally keep still. It may be easier to spot the effects of a large scale infestation - yellowing and dropping leaves, and twig dieback. The presence of sooty mold is also usually a clear sign of scale infestation.

Organic Control Methods

Oil sprays: Spraying the plant with white oil acts to both control the scale and loosen the sooty mold, which will then wash off more easily. The best time to spray is during the immature 'crawler' stage of the scale. This is usually around midsummer, and is often indicated by increased ant activity around the plant. White oil and other oil sprays work to suffocate scale insects at all stages of the life-cycle.

Soap sprays: Potassium-based insecticidal soap sprays are also a good alternative to controlling the scale because they dissolve the insects' outer coating, causing it to dehydrate. Both soap and oil-sprays have little-to-no impact on the garden's beneficial insects.

Other sprays: Sprays made from garlic or pyrethrum may also be used successfully to shield plants against scale infestation.

Horticultural glue: Use a horticultural glue to keep ants out of your trees. This will make it a lot easier for the wasps to parasitize the scale.

Clean up: As an additional measure, cut long grass around the trunk and prune any twigs or branches that touch the ground since ants may use these as bridges.
Prune heavily infested twigs from garden plants. To avoid spreading the scale, drop these twigs in soapy water before mulching or placing them in the compost.

Tree bands: Grease bands around the trunks of the trees also act to prevent ants from climbing up.

Natural predators: If you make your garden a welcoming and nourishing environment for the natural predators of scale, you will reap the benefits for years to come.

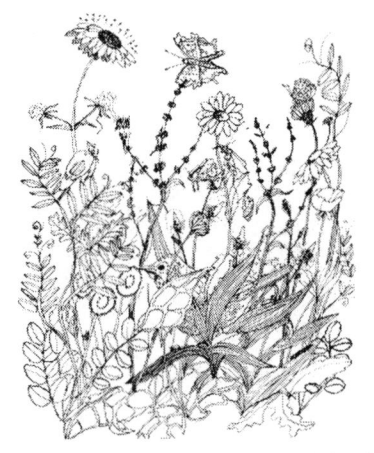

Insectary flowers attract beneficial insects and birds to your garden

Scale's natural enemies include ladybeetles, lacewings, spiders and miniscule parasitoid wasps. Most of the helpful insects that destroy garden pests need nectar and pollen for sustenance during a period of their lifecycle. Furthermore, they are usually quite small, with correspondingly small mouthparts, which means they are only able to feed on specific flowers with the right characteristics. If you provide a bountiful supply of food these garden helpers will live longer and produce more offspring.

Grow a constant, twelve-month supply of the right kinds of flowers, and you will support beneficial insect populations throughout the year. Plant a mixture of 'insectary plants' such as red clover, alyssum, cosmos, marigolds, Queen Anne's Lace, buckwheat, lucerne, dill, caraway, coriander, phacelia and gypsophila. These plants flower for most of the year, offering nectar, pollen and habitat for a range of helpful insects such as predatory mites, micro wasps, ladybeetles, lacewings, hoverflies, tachnid flies and predatory beetles.
Birds can also help control scale population. Make sure your garden is bird-friendly by providing sources of water and nesting sites, and by keeping cats indoors or belled.

SAN JOSE SCALE

The San Jose scale (*Quadraspidiotus perniciosus*) is a small, yellow, pear-shaped insect which feeds on tree sap. It hides, as an adult, under a gray, waxy scale of up to 2 mm in length. They often hide in crevices, cracks in bark, forks of branches and in the space between bud and stem. Colonies of such scales may form encrustations on tree branches, often with a similar color and texture to the bark. They affect many fruit trees, including pears and almonds.

Sign of infestation: The San Jose scale both feeds on sap and slowly poisons the tree by secreting poisonous substances into the plant cells. As a result, the bark begins to crack, and the surrounding branches die back. If untreated, the whole plant may die.

Organic control methods: Prune the infested branches and twigs from the tree. Spray the pruned branches, then burn or otherwise dispose of them far from where they do any harm.
White oil (also known as winter oil) can be sprayed onto the trees and fruit. Be sure to drench the tree thoroughly. Do not spray near spring - only within the dormant season.
Biological controls include ladybeetles, chalcid and aphelinid wasps.

San Jose Scale

THRIPS

Thrips are tiny insect pests that affect many fruit trees, including citrus and pears. Only about 1 mm long, they feed on developing plant tissue such as blossoms, young foliage and shoots. The larvae are white, and marked on the undersides with a ring of dark spines. The young insects are light yellow in color, but as they mature they darken to a brown-black.

Lifecycle: Adult female thrips spend the winter dormant in the soil, emerging in early spring to feed. Once they have found a 'host' (young plant tissue in the leaves, petioles, blossoms and fruit buds) the female lays her eggs. These eggs take up to a week to hatch into instar larvae. There are two instar iterations - the second one ends in summer, where the larva falls from the tree into the leaf litter and creates an underground cell in which to pupate. Pupation occurs in autumn.

Signs of Infestation

Thrips can cause damage to blossoms, leaves, fruit buds and shoots - causing them to develop abnormally or die. Damaged buds can be identified by the drops of gum that form on them - telltale signs of a thrips infestation. On fruit in which the thrips sometimes lay their eggs, tiny russet indents form at the site of each egg puncture. Defoliation may occur, causing stunted growth and weakness.

Organic Control Methods

Thrips have many natural predators, including lacewings, lady beetles and pirate bugs. These can be encouraged by growing insect-attracting flowers such as clover beneath your fruit trees. Spinosad sprays can also be effective.

TWO-SPOTTED MITE

Two spotted mites are minuscule organisms that feed on the chlorophyll in plant leaves. For most of the year they are a yellow-green color (with the two spots on their back that gives them the name), and in the autumn they turn red. Because of their infinitesimal size (around half a millimetre) they are difficult to spot. Instead, a gardener's first sign of two-spotted mite is when the surfaces of the leaves start to display a white spotting pattern (where the chlorophyll has been eaten). They affect many plants - from pears to apples, nuts, vegetables, stonefruit and berries.

Signs of Infestation

Since chlorophyll is essential for the plant's conversion of sunlight into energy, mite infestations reduce the vigour of the tree. They can cause defoliation and widespread yellowing of leaves.

Organic Control Methods

Two spotted mites have some natural enemies, including the predatory mites Phytoseiulus persimilis and Typhlodromus occidentalist, as well as hoverflies, lacewings, damsel bugs and predatory thrips. Try and attract these insects by planting insectary flowers and spreading mulch. Mulch is good shelter for ground-dwelling insects.

Using a high pressure hose in the morning for three consecutive days can help dislodge the mites.

White oil is an effective and safe spray, as are insecticidal soap sprays and pyrethrum sprays.

2
APPLES AND CRABAPPLES

APPLE SCAB

Apple scab is a common disease affecting apple and crabapple trees. It causes spotting ('scabbing') of the fruit, particularly during wet spring weather which fuels the growth of the fungus that causes it.

The offending party is the fungus *Venturia inaequalis*, which grows and is spread through fallen and decaying leaves and fruit. The fungus causes a serious disease in apple and crabapple trees, resulting in blemishing of the fruit and, in some cases, a complete loss of the crop. As mentioned above, it is most severe in cool, moist weather; it happens to afflict trees grown in coastal areas more than those grown inland.

Signs of Infection

Apple scab first presents as yellow ('chlorotic') spots on apple tree leaves. As the disease progresses, dark spots form on the leaves, the fruit, and sometimes even the stems. The lower leaves (which are affected first) may take on a blister-like appearance. If you turn them over, you may find that their undersurface has a sheen to it; this is due to the fungal growth that has occurred. You may find the leaves in a twisted or puckered state. If you've caught it early, only a few scattered leaves will be affected, but in a further progressed state, literally all the foliage will be affected. Once the disease reaches its apex, the leaves will often turn become yellowed and drop off the tree.

Similarly, when scab has reached the stems, the flowers are also liable to drop off. Spots – the scabs themselves – usually develop on the fruit later in the season. Beginning with the velvety sheen mentioned above, in time the scabs may acquire sooty, gray-black lesions with a halo of red around them.

Once these lesions run their course, they can severely infect the fruit, causing it to become misshapen and fall from the tree. Additional pest organisms may become involved once the fruit cracks, giving these small invaders an opening. Pears may also be affected by scab disease – their skins becoming deformed by black, sunken lesions that distort the fruit.

Apple scab can devastate an apple crop. Infected flowers and fruit will often drop early; the apples can become virtually inedible due to the malformation and blemishing scabs cause.

Temperature is an important variant in apple scab infection. It occurs most rapidly when the temperature hovers between 55 and 75 degrees Fahrenheit; in order for infection to occur, the leaves or fruit must remain moist continuously for about nine hours. When warmer weather is also dry, apple scab is typically less prevalent.

APPLE SCAB DISEASE CYCLE

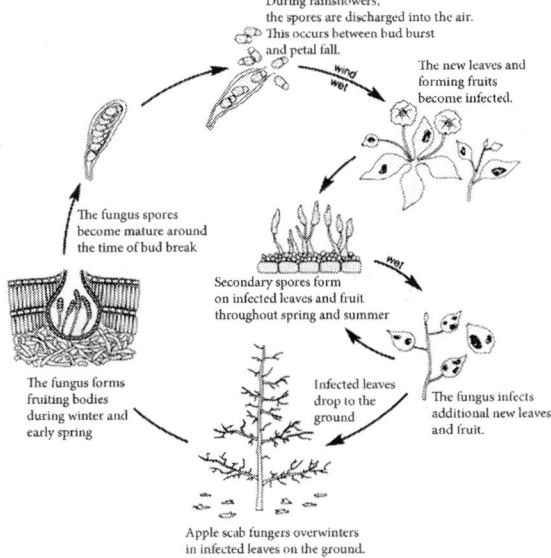

Diagram courtesy of Cornell University.

Life Cycle: The apple scab pathogen spends the winter feeding off infected leaves that have fallen to the ground. In warmer weather, rainfall, splashing water and air currents cause the spores to be released and become airborne. At that point, the fungal infection spreads from the leaves on the ground to the flowers, leaves, and fruit; there, they germinate and cause secondary infections.

Organic Control Methods

Sanitation: The simplest method of curing apple scab is the removal and composting of dropped leaves; this is the ideal solution for one or two trees in a yard or garden.
With a larger number of trees, further steps are usually required, especially in groves located in coastal areas or where the weather is moist and cool.

Nitrogen and lime: Natural sources of nitrogen (such as fertilizer urea) and zinc may be applied to the leaves in the fall (autumn); these will cause the affected leaves to fall before infection of the stem and fruit can occur. Applying lime to the leaves that gather beneath the tree can also be highly effective and halting the advance of the disease.

Timing of irrigation: Because moisture is so central to apple scab development, it is important to irrigate or water early in the day, allowing time for the leaves to dry before nightfall. The sprinkler's angle can be altered to allow for ideal drying.

Choosing resistant cultivars: In addition, there are naturally scab-resistant varieties of apple and crabapple trees that can be chosen to take the place of more disease-susceptible strains. In Australia, an organically-grown scab-resistant apple has been bred, with considerable success, at an experimental site in

Queensland. (For more information on this breed, see 'RS103-130' in the Department of Primary Industries and Fisheries, Queensland.)

Wood ash: Scab fungus flourishes on the acidic surfaces of leaves and fruit. Sprinkling wood ash onto the leaves of infected apple trees increases the alkalinity, reducing the spread of the disease.

Lime spray: Spraying the trees with a solution of builder's lime mixed with water can also achieve the same effect. Only a small amount is needed every season. To make the solution, mix a handful of builder's lime with water to create a 'milk' and spray it over the canopies of the trees.

CODLING MOTH

One common apple pest is the codling moth, which is covered in General Fruit Pests and Diseases.

POWDERY MILDEW

Powdery mildew is another common fungal disease that strikes apples, along with strawberries and grapes. It is most prevalent in warm, moist environments. The pathogen that causes it is called *Podosphaera leucotricha*; it is a parasite that attacks the live tissue of plants. It spreads from one plant to neighboring plants, and can be devastating to apple crops.

Signs of Infection

When a plant is infected with powdery mildew, a white, powdery substance forms on the upper surface of low-hanging leaves. As in an apple scab infection, leaves may become twisted and deformed, dying and falling from the tree.

Infected shoots become silvery-gray in color; they cause stunted fruit growth and general defoliation. Once infected, a tree can experience considerable spread quickly, which weakens it and makes it more susceptible to secondary infections. Powdery mildew can significantly affect both fruit yield and quality.

The period between spore germination and the formation of new spores may be as short as 48 hours. Humidity is a major factor: when it's high, spore formation is favoured, while low humidity encourages spore dispersal.

Some powdery mildews are increased by free-standing moisture on leaves; other strains, by wetness on leaf surfaces.

Organic Control Methods

Humidity control: Accumulating moisture feeds the pathogens and allows for reinfection. Don not water your fruit plants from above; instead, water the soil. Improve air circulation by thinning and pruning your fruit trees. If you have control over overnight humidity – that is to say, if you're growing your fruit in a greenhouse – you can drive off water by ventilating and heating the greenhouse just before twilight.

Sanitation: Remove and destroy all infected plant parts.

Withhold ferilizer: Do not fertilize your fruit plants until the problem is corrected. Powdery mildew favors young, succulent growth.

Apply a fungicide: There are many organic fungicides available. Check the label to be sure they are safe and effective on the type of plant that is infected. Look for ingredients such as: potassium bicarbonate, neem oil, sulfur or copper. See also our section on home-made fungicides.

Most fungicides will need repeat applications every 7 - 14 days, for continuous protection. Always follow the label instructions for both application and waiting period before harvest.

LIGHT BROWN APPLE MOTH

The light brown apple moth is a significant pest that targets pome fruit like apples, and is covered above in the chapter on General Fruit Pests and Diseases.

BROWN ROT

Monilinia fructigena is a virulent fungal disease known as brown rot. This afflicts fruits, leaves, and blossoms in equal measure. The evidence for brown rot infection is the presence of concentric circles of fungal growth around the apple. *M. fructigena* can cause considerable damage to apple yields.
The pathogen is not indigenous to Australia, so infections are almost always the result of illegal plant imports. (Two other Monilinia strains that do occur naturally in Western Australia are *Monilia fructicola* and *Monolinia laxa*.)

Signs of Infection

Circular, brown bands tend to form on the fruit during a brown rot infection. These bands indicate the soft decay that is occurring under the surface of the fruit. The fungal growths spread to the twigs of the plant, resulting in the wilting of shoots, as well as cankers. Diseased fruit tend not to fall to the ground; rather, they hang on, resulting in shoot dieback.

The *M. fructigena* fungus can overwinter on diseased fruit – both on the ground below the tree and while still attached. The infected fruit is particularly likely to produce spores when conditions are favourable; that is, during moist and warm weather. The spores are carried on the wind or by the movements of insects. The points of infection tend to be open wounds, scab lesions, or where insect damage is already present.

Organic Control Methods

- Prevention is the key to controlling brown rot infection.
- When possible, plant *M. fructigena*-resistant fruit cultivars.
- Promptly remove and destroy infected plant tissue. This procedure should break the life cycle of brown rot in individual trees, and may keep future infestation beneath fruit-threatening levels.
- Be sure to remove any infected fruit and other parts of the tree that have fallen to the ground.
- Regular pruning will encourage healthy air circulation.
- Watering the tree at its base only will prevent the accumulation of moisture on the foliage and fruit, which in turn will prevent future brown rot infestations.
- Organic fungicides such as copper and sulfur sprays and powders can be applied as frequently as once per week. Begin this process when the first blossoms become visible and continue thereafter until the growing season comes to an end. Sulfur and copper sprays do not kill the fungus; instead, they inhibit the fungal spore germination process.

WOOLY APHIDS

The wooly aphid is an insect pest known as *Eriosoma lanigerum*. Its mandibles pierce and suck the fruit, making it a formidable apple tree pest. As adults, wooly aphids are predominantly wingless and female.

Their common name derives from the white, waxy excretions they carry all over their bodies as a form of protection from predators. The adults are about 2mm long and their waxy coating makes them look white.

Signs of Infestation

Woolly aphids imbibe tree sap, targeting new, thin, or damaged growth areas. Parts of the tree that have been extensively pruned or which have sections of broken bark are particularly subject to aphid attacks.

Where the insects bore into the wood, it tends to become gnarled, bumpy and malformed. Fruit tends to fall early and/or become visibly misshapen. The gnarled appearance of the wood may reach as far down as the root system; youthful trees infested with wooly aphids may fail to grow to their expected size. A secondary problem often presents: the presence of aphids is often associated with outbreaks of the sooty mold fungus.

Organic Control Methods

Natural predators: The wasp species *Aphelinus mali* is your friend when it comes to wooly aphid infestations. This species is parasitic on aphids; adult A. mali inject their larvae into aphids and these literally consume the insect from the inside out. Be certain you're not using any pesticides or other chemicals harmful to these friendly wasps, so as to conserve them and keep the aphid population under control.

Other natural predators of wooly aphids include syrphid fly larvae, ladybeetles, and lacewing larvae. These beneficial insects can be attracted by planting flowers and herbs such as alyssum, scabius, fennel, dill, coreopsis, yarrow, lupins or sunflowers beneath the trees.
Planting nasturtiums at the base of the trees may help prevent wooly aphids from crawling up the trunk.

Rootstock selection: Try to obtain and use Northern Spy and Malling-Merton rootstock, both of which are naturally resistant to aphid infestation. M793 and Northern Spy are particularly resistant.

Keep trees healthy: Also, avoid mowing grass close to the apple tree trunk in case you accidentally damage the bark. Use an antifungal sealant on any wounds. Try to do most of your pruning in the summer – wounds heal more quickly in warmer weather. Keep the tree and surrounding garden healthy through watering well, and applying a balanced fertilizer, mulch and manure to the soil.

Sprays: Organic sprays can be used on fruit trees to combat aerial populations of wooly aphid. Oil sprays (such as Eco-Oil, paraffin oil, winter oil or white oil) will smother the aphids and dehydrate the eggs. Similarly, lime sulfur can be sprayed into bark fissures to kill hard-to-reach eggs. Apply during the winter months.

Methylated spirits: Gardening guru Peter Cundall says that wooly aphids: '… attack apple trees and, in the winter, they congregate all the way around, mainly where the main graft is. They look like cottonwool, and they can do massive damage. There's a cure and this is it, and it's not water, this is methylated spirits. I use an old paintbrush, poured on like that, soaked on, doesn't matter if a bit goes on the ground, and there it is, you paint them all the way round, like that. Soak the stuff in there and you can hear them squealing in the night. It's brilliant stuff.'

Manual removal: Squashing the white fluffy substances on the tree will kill the aphids hiding within. However the aphids in the roots will not be affected, nor will it prevent the aphid eggs from hatching.

Woolly aphid adult

3

AVOCADOS

The avocado (*Persea americana*) is a tree native to Mexico and Central America. 'Avocado' or 'alligator pear' also refers to the fruit, botanically a large berry that contains a single seed.

Avocados are commercially valuable and are cultivated in tropical and Mediterranean climates throughout the world. They have a green-skinned, fleshy body that may be pear-shaped, egg-shaped, or spherical. Commercially, they ripen after harvesting.

Trees are partially self-pollinating and often are propagated through grafting to maintain a predictable quality and quantity of the fruit.

Source: Wikipedia

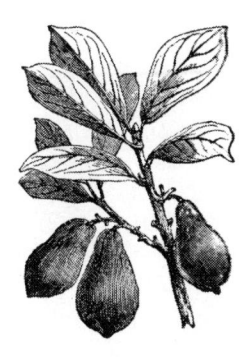

AVOCADO RED MITE

Avocado Red Mite (*Oligonychus yothersi*) is the avocado plant's most common insect predator. At first, its feeding is confined to the uppermost surface of the leaves; it then proceeds along the midrib by way of secondary leaf veins.

Signs of Infestation

Affected areas become rust-colored along the veins of the leaf. Heavy red mite infestations can stymie up to 30% of the plant's photosynthetic activity. As a result, leaves fall prematurely and fruit quality is impacted.

Organic Control Methods

Relatively few organic miticides are recommended for use on avocado plants when they are bearing fruit. Instead, apply sulfur spray or oil emulsion sprays.

FRUIT-SPOTTING BUG

The fruit-spotting bug, a common avocado pest, is covered in more detail in the chapter on General Fruit Pests and Diseases.

MIRID BUG

Mirid bugs have been known to target avocado trees in Queensland. See the chapter 'General Fruit Pests and Diseases'.

ANTHRACNOSE

Avocados can be affected by anthracnose. See 'anthracnose' in the chapter on 'General Fruit Pests and Diseases'.

4

BANANAS

Banana plants are, strictly speaking herbs, not woody fruit trees. Although all bananas belong to the genus Musa, different varieties have different sizes, shapes and firmness.

Depending on variety, ripe banana rinds may may be purple, red, green, brown or (most commonly) yellow.

BANANA BUNCHY TOP VIRUS (BBTV)

Signs of Infection

Banana bunchy top virus is characterised by dark green flecks on leaf-veins, in a 'dot-dash' pattern. These are easiest to spot on the underside of the leaf, near the base. Vein-flecking can also be present on the leaf-sheaths and petioles. The vigour of the plant is reduced, with 'bunching' of the leaves occurring. The leaves may start to exhibit wavy yellow margins. Depending on when infection occurred, stunting of the plant may prevent the formation of banana bunches, or distort the young 'fruit'.

Organic Control Methods

Unfortunately there is no cure for BBTV, and as with all viral diseases, the infected plants must be promptly destroyed. In the case of this viral disease (given the Australian banana industry and fears of how this disease could, if spread, cause severe destruction to the industry), you must notify the authorities as quarantine restrictions apply, and removal of infected plants must be conducted by a trained inspector. See the Plant Protection Act 1989 for more information.

PANAMA DISEASE

Panama disease is caused by the fungus *Fusarium oxysporum f.sp. Cubense*.

Signs of Infection

Panama disease is characterised by a yellowing and withering at the edges of the leaves, which eventually turn completely brown, drooping to form a 'skirt' of dying leaves around the stump of the plant. The stem may split, exhibiting discoloration of the water-conducting tissue. Fruit is damaged or non-existent.

Organic Control Methods

Many parts of the world are entirely free of certain aggressive forms of Panama disease, such as tropical race 4. National governments in conjunction with the banana industry are extremely concerned with the possibility of the spread of disease - therefore to help prevent a deadly outbreak that could devastate the banana industry (and for the sake of your own plants) stay constantly alert to the health of your plants, and if they display any symptoms of this disease, you must contact your local authorities so they can come and contain a possible outbreak. Do not try to treat Panama Disease on your own.

ANTHRACNOSE

Anthracnose - see the chapter 'General Fruit Pests and Diseases'.

BANANA LEAF RUST

(*Uredo musae* and *Uromyces musae*)

Signs of Infection

These fungal pathogens cause a rusty appearance on leaves.

Organic Control Methods

Spray with an organic fungicide. See the chapters on 'Homemade Remedies' and 'Commercial Remedies'.

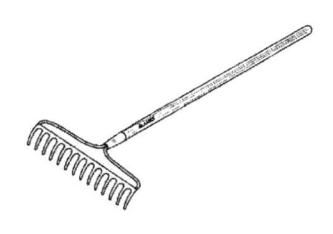

BANANA LEAF SPECKLE

(*Acrodontium simplex*)

Signs of Infection

A speckled appearance on leaves.

Organic Control Methods

Spray with an organic fungicide. See the chapters on 'Homemade Remedies' and 'Commercial Remedies'.

CROWN ROT

(*Fusarium pallidoroseum, Colletotrichum musae, Verticillium theobromae, Fusarium spp., Acremonium spp.*)

Crown rot is more of a problem for commercial banana growers than home gardener, because it generally affects bananas during shipping.

Signs of Infection

Crown rot affects the 'crown' (the top) of a bunch of bananas that unites the fruit. Symptoms appear after the bananas have been cut, and is characterised by fungal growths on the crown, blackened patches on the fruit, and early ripening.

Organic Control Methods

Organic fungicides, plastic sleeving and breeding susceptibility out of the genes are all methods that are being used to combat crown rot. See the chapters on 'Homemade Remedies' and 'Commercial Remedies'.

FRUIT SPECKLE

(Deightoniella torulosa)

Signs of Infection

Black speckles on the skin of the banana fruit.

Organic Control Methods

Spray with an organic fungicide. See the chapters on 'Homemade Remedies' and 'Commercial Remedies'.

YELLOW SIGATOKA

Yellow Sigatoka leaf spot is a fungal disease that affects the Cavendish banana variety, usually in commercial settings. Since the fungus flourishes in hot, wet conditions, it is most common in northern Queensland.

Signs of Infection

Yellow Sigatoka can be identified by the appearance of tiny yellow streaks on the leaves (1-2mm long), which develop and enlarge to become black ovoid spots up to 10mm long. Over time these spots turn gray and are bordered with black and a yellow 'halo'. Eventually, if the disease runs unchecked, large dead patches will form on the leaves.

This fungal disease has the potential to severely defoliate the plant, weakening the tree and thus reducing yield.

Organic Control Methods

The disease can be controlled elsewhere in Australia (other than in northern Queensland) by the correct use of organic fungicides. See also our section on homemade fungicides.

BANANA-SPOTTING BUG

(Amblypelta lutescens lutescens)

Although the banana-spotting bug is known best for attacking banana plants, it also targets avocados, custard apples, passionfruit, pawpaws, guavas and other plants. It is closely related to the fruit-spotting bug, which is covered in the chapter 'General Fruit Pests and Diseases'.

Lifecycle: Banana-spotting bugs go through several life stages, beginning as tiny green triangular eggs, laid singly on the leaves, flowers or fruit. After hatching, the bug goes through five nymphal stages - from reddish-brown, antlike creatures (with antennae displaying a flattened joint) and white-ringed scent glands on the abdomen. As they progress through the nymphal stages the bugs will turn greener, and develop wingbuds. The adult bug is yellowish green, and is about 15mm in length.

Signs of Infestation

The bugs feed by piercing the plant tissue and sucking the nutrients. As a result, they cause significant tissue damage around the feeding site - resulting in sunken black lesions at bite spots. Most banana-spotting bug activity occurs from mid-spring to late autumn.

Damage from the banana-spotting bug often causes the plant to shed young fruit. Maturer fruit may survive, but will be distorted, 'dimpled' and damaged. The damage appears similar to that of the Queensland fruit fly (another general pest) - to determine whether the culprit is the fruit fly or the banana-spotting bug, cut into the wound on the plant and try to find white eggs or maggots. If none can be found, it is most likely a banana/fruit-spotting bug and not the fruit fly.

Organic Control Methods

Examine five trees at each of six widely spaced locations throughout the crop. Spray with organic pesticide when damage is noted. Apart from positioning the orchard as far as possible from uncleared scrub areas, little can be done to alleviate bug incidence. Egg parasites are being investigated for biological control of these pests. Green tree ants and assassin bugs can exert considerable control.

Considerable fruit damage may result from the feeding of a relatively small number of bugs that are difficult to detect on the tree. Orchard history and experience dictate the frequency of organic pesticide sprays applied to control the pest. Sprays need to be applied every 2, 3, or 4 weeks depending on the orchard's location and history of attack. Ensure thorough coverage. Mature orchards with touching canopies should be thinned to facilitate spraying as well as to increase the area of fruiting canopy.

BURROWING NEMATODE

(*Radopholus similis*)

Burrowing nematode affects hundreds of plant varieties in tropical and subtropical areas. Types of plants affected include bananas, citruses, ginger, coconut and black pepper. These miniscule pests are microscopic, colorless worms that burrow into a plant's root system to feed, thus damaging their ability to take in water or nutrients.

Signs of Infestation

As burrowing nematodes are so tiny, and their activity takes place underground, they are often difficult to detect. Often the first signs of damage (stunted growth, decreased vigor, smaller delayed fruit, wilting and leaf-drop) may be taken for a lack of watering or insufficient fertilization. In bananas, the nematodes will eventually destroy the anchor roots, increasing the likelihood of plant-toppling. Roots will start to show reddish-brown lesions, and black spots may appear on the rhizome.

Organic Control Methods

Eradicating burrowing nematodes from the soil is difficult - involving the removal not only of the host plant and all its roots but the removal of all weeds and other hosts. This will starve the nematodes and they will eventually die off. After this period, the patch of land should be left fallow for 12 months, or planed with a nematode-suppressor crop. An expensive alternative method is to flood the soil for eight weeks.

BANANA APHID

Banana aphids are small reddish-brown to black insects with two projections from the abdomen. Their damage from feeding or from the sooty mold that often builds up as a result of the honeydew excretions is rarely significant. Banana aphids are a major concern however because they are known vectors of the devastating banana bunchy-top virus (see Banana Diseases).

Can be controlled by the careful and regular use of organic pesticides such as white oil and insecticidal soap.. Commercial organic pesticides for control of aphids include Diatomaceous Earth, Absorbacide and Amgrow Tomato and Vegetable Dust. General purpose organic pest controls include Beat-A-Bug Insect Spray, Eco-Oil, Natrasoap and Orange Guard Crawling Insect Spray.

See also the chapters on 'Homemade Remedies' and 'Commercial Remedies'.

BANANA FLOWER THRIPS

The tiny, straw-colored slender thrips cause damage by feeding on and laying eggs on fruit skins, causing raised areas of corky scab.

Can be controlled by the careful and regular use of organic pesticides such as white oil and insecticidal soap. Commercial organic pesticides for control of thrips include Diatomaceous Earth, Absorbacide and Amgrow Tomato and Vegetable Dust. General purpose organic pest controls include Beat-A-Bug Insect Spray, Eco-Oil, Natrasoap and Orange Guard Crawling Insect Spray.

BANANA FRUIT CATERPILLAR

Banana fruit caterpillars are large, gray-brown nymphs of the moth Tiracola plagiata. The caterpillars can grow to 60mm long, and feed on the banana fruit. Instead of merely feeding on the rind, these pest burrow deep into the fruit, rendering it inedible. A few caterpillars can destroy an entire bunch.

Can be controlled by the careful and regular use of organic pesticides. Commercial organic pesticides for caterpillar and moth control include Dipel, EcoGrub, Insect Hotel and Success.
General purpose organic pest controls include Beat-A-Bug Insect Spray, Eco-Oil, Natrasoap and Orange Guard Crawling Insect Spray.

BANANA RUST THRIPS AND BANANA-SILVERING THRIPS

Banana rust and banana-silvering thrips are yellow to golden-brown in color, and 1.5mm long. They feed and lay eggs beneath the surface of the fruit skin, causing either a raised, rusty discoloration or a silvery blemish. Eating quality is not adversely affected.

Can be controlled by the careful and regular use of organic pesticides such as white oil and insecticidal soap. Commercial organic pesticides for control of thrips include Diatomaceous Earth, Absorbacide and Amgrow Tomato and Vegetable Dust. General purpose organic pest controls include Beat-A-Bug Insect Spray, Eco-Oil, Natrasoap and Orange Guard Crawling Insect Spray.

BANANA SCAB MOTH

The banana scab moth is a small (25mm) brown and black-spotted moth, the larvae of which feed on immature bananas, causing black calloused scars on the skin (but rarely affecting the fruit inside).

Can be controlled by the careful and regular use of organic pesticides. See the chapters on 'Homemade Remedies' and 'Commercial Remedies'.

BANANA WEEVIL BORER

Signs of Infestation

The larvae of the banana weevil borer tunnel into the plant's corm, weakening it and interfering with the uptake of water and nutrients. This makes the plant more susceptible to being blown down. As adults, the banana weevil is dull black, around 10-12mm long. Larvae are white, wormlike and swollen in the middle. Their heads are brown.

Organic Control Methods

A large range of general predators including ants and beneficial beetles assist in reducing banana weevil borer numbers. Can also be controlled by the careful and regular use of organic pesticides. See the chapters on 'Homemade Remedies' and 'Commercial Remedies'.

FRUIT-SPOTTING BUGS

See the chapter 'General Fruit Pests and Diseases'.

CLUSTER CATERPILLAR

The cluster caterpillar feeds the leaves of many host plants, including bananas, beans and sunflowers. Their damage usually does not significantly affect the plant. They are the larvae of the moth Spodoptera litura, which have brown wings crossed with cream streaks.

Signs of Infestation

The larvae go through four instar stages. The first instars are light green, with a darker thorax. They cluster together to feed. The second instar sports a red, yellow and green pattern of lines on the back, a dark spot behind the head and a row of dark spots along both sides - while the third instar is brown with black dots down the sides, and three pale lines and a row of dark 'half-moon' shapes down the back. The final instar can be over 50mm long, and is dark brown.

No control is required, since leaf damage is mostly cosmetic and the plant quickly compensates by producing new leaves. Fruit damage is rare and usually confined to a few bunches only.

Fruit-Piercing Moth

See the chapter 'General Fruit Pests and Diseases'

Queensland Fruit Fly

See the chapter 'General Fruit Pests and Diseases'.

Two-spotted Spider Mite

See the chapter 'General Fruit Pests and Diseases'.

Spiralling Whitefly

Spiralling whiteflies are minuscule insects (0.2mm long) which form colonies of adults and nymphs on the undersides of leaves. These colonies are protected by a highly visible coating of wax and honeydew, which takes the form of lumpy white spots surrounded by a tangled spiralling white patch. Sooty mold often accompanies this pest.

Can be controlled by the careful and regular use of organic pesticides. Commercial organic pesticides for control of whitefly include Diatomaceous Earth, Absorbacide and Amgrow Tomato and Vegetable Dust.

General purpose organic pest controls include Beat-A-Bug Insect Spray, Eco-Oil, Natrasoap and Orange Guard Crawling Insect Spray.

Also see the chapters on 'Homemade Remedies' and 'Commercial Remedies'.

Sugarcane bud moth

Signs of Infestation

The sugarcane bud moth (*Opogona glycyphaga*) is a small (10mm long) yellow-and-purple moth with feathery hindwings. The larvae feed on the skin of immature banana fruits, causing superficial scarring.

Organic Control Methods

Organic remedies include insecticidal soap and white oil. General purpose organic pest controls include Beat-A-Bug Insect Spray, Eco-Oil, Natrasoap and Orange Guard Crawling Insect Spray. Commercial organic pesticides for caterpillar and moth control include Dipel, EcoGrub, Insect Hotel and Success.

Sugarcane bud moth

5

BERRIES

BERRIES

The botanical definition of a berry is a fleshy fruit produced from a single ovary. In everyday English, however, 'berry' is a term for any small edible fruit.

'Berry' fruits are usually juicy, round, brightly colored, sweet or sour. They generally do not have a stone or pit, although many seeds may be present.

In this sense it includes the Rubus genus (boysenberries, silvanberries, cloudberries, jostaberries, raspberries, salmonberries, blackberries etc.), the Ribes genus (blackcurrants, redcurrants, whitecurrants, gooseberries and jostaberries, which are a hybrid of gooseberries and black currants), Fragaria (strawberries), and the Vaccinium genus (blueberries, bilberries and cranberries).

Gooseberries and currants both belong to the Ribes family. Gooseberries will grow in temperate to subtropical conditions. Black currants however require winter chilling and will only yield good crops in cold environments. Both berries are popular in cooking and jams, but have a tart flavor when fresh.

(Hint: plant blackcurrants in a slightly acidic, well-drained soil – around 6-6.5 pH).

Some of the more unusual berries include goji, chokecherry, Chilean guava, goumi, Macqui, honeyberry, sea buckthorn, bearberry, acerola, crowberry, appleberry, snowberry, Chinese bayberry, calafate, sapodilla, Surinam cherry, saskatoon and Juneberry.

AMERICAN GOOSEBERRY MILDEW

Gooseberry mildew is a serious fungal disease caused by the imported American mildew *Sphaerotheca mors-uvae*. It more commonly attacks in wet conditions. If unchecked, it can severely damage plants and completely destroy crops.

Signs of Infestation

Emerging foliage typically exhibits the first signs of this disease. If the new leaves are lime green instead of the healthy deep green color, then the plant has been infected. In advanced cases the leaves fail to expand, and appear covered in a white powdery substance. Fruit may fail to set, and those which do are small, thick-skinned and dusted with mildew.

Organic Control Methods

Spraying the plant with an organic fungicide is the only real solution to this debilitating disease.

CURRANT BORER MOTH

Signs of Infestation

The larvae of this moth bore into the stems of the blackcurrant, creating wide, deep tunnels.

Organic Control Methods

Pruning the infested stems is currently the only known method of controlling the borer moth.

STRAWBERRY BLACK ROOT ROT

Black root rot is a disease caused by a pathogenic fungus (*Thielaviopsis basicola*) in the soil. Most older strawberry plantings or re-plantings are typically affected.

Signs of Infection

The symptoms of this disease include a patchy appearance among the strawberries. The best indicator of Thielaviopsis basicola infection is a brown appearance on the normally white (or tan) areas on the roots.

When infected by *T. basicola*, the rootlets of berry-producing tree tend to become black and deteriorate. As the infection spreads, the entire root becomes fragile enough to break off easily when bent. Trees affected by black root rot will become stunted and produce far fewer berries than a healthy plant.

Organic Control Methods

Black root rot is associated with soils with relatively high clay content. An excellent preventive measure is to plant in soils that are both well-drained and well-aerated. Choosing soils with fairly high organic is also quite helpful. Avoid soil compaction and excessive irrigation.

Over-winter mulching can greatly reduce injury.

Purchasing uninfected plants is a must. Rotating berry crops every three to five years can help keep black rot populations under control.

RASPBERRY CANE SPOT

Cane Spot, also known as anthracnose (*Elsinoe veneta*), is an infection that strikes raspberry crops. It can be particularly serious when rains continue late into spring.
See also 'anthracnose' in 'General Pests'.

Signs of Infection on Raspberries

The cane spots caused by anthracnose retard sap flow, girdling the canes. Infected canes may result in uneven ripening of the fruit. Infections usually begin on the lower portions of the cane toward the inside of the plant; it often proceeds to the fruit and the leaves.

Initially, small reddish-purple circles appear on the cane; as they grow in size, they cause sinking and cracking in the center of the cane. The affected patches tend to cluster and merge, forming large, irregular portions. Eventually, the canes will become girdled and die.

Depending on which raspberry variety you've planted, the leaves and stems may exhibit purple spotting. The berries may ripen unevenly and produce unusually small drupelets. Infections occurring early in the growing season tend to do more damage than those late-season infections.

Organic Control Methods

Sanitation: To control anthracnose on raspberries, it is essential to rake rake up and remove all infected leaves. Prune away all the dead wood and burn it.

Site choice: Avoid planting susceptible strains of raspberries in regions with heavy spring rain and/or fog.

Plant health: If you plant raspberries in areas where the summers are hot, or where drought is a factor, you should deeply irrigate the berries monthly.

Preventative sprays: Neem Oil (70%) is an excellent fungicide and an effective preventative. Neem Oil should be applied to the affected plants over the course of two weeks, as a preventive measure.

Anti-fungal sprays: To kill established fungi, apply liquid copper fungicide.

RASPBERRY BOTRYTIS

Signs of Infection

Botrytis fruit rot (*Botrytis cinerea*) is found on the flowers and fruit of raspberries and is more prevalent during warm, moist autumns. On flowers, the fungus will cause the blooms to either wither and brown (in dry conditions) or become covered with gray fungal tufts (in wet conditions).

Immature fruit will turn purplish-gray and hard while mature fruit (especially overripe and bruised fruit) develop soft, spreading, light brown patches that spread to shrivel the berry and cover it in gray fuzz.

The stems of infected berries may also become infected, 'blasting' (turning brown and withering) downward from the fruit. In summer, the leaves and canes may develop brown lesions. In autumn and winter these cane lesions take the form of tan, concentric 'watermarks'.

Botrytis fruit rot may also infect previously-healthy harvested fruit, especially if bruised or wet berries are left out in warm conditions.

Organic Control Methods

* Spray with organic approved copper-based fungicide. Spraying the plant should not just be a curative measure but a protectant one. During the early flowering stage, before any fungus could have taken hold, spray at least twice with a fungicide (with 14 days between each spray). The plants may need additional spraying later on during the fruiting season, depending on the weather and whether a fungus infection has indeed taken hold. It is recommended that you alternate between at least two types of fungicide to prevent the fungi becoming resistant to one.

* Be sure to prune and trellis the canes to encourage air circulation and prevent prolonged moist environments for the fungus to develop. Clear around the plants by weeding and burning back the primocanes.

* Adjustment of your irrigation may also be necessary to prevent extended moist conditions on the plant.

* The botrytis fungus infects new green growth with particular ease, so avoid the excessive use of nitrogen fertilizer in springtime.

* To prevent botrytis from infecting the harvest, pick the fruit before they reach full maturity. Instead of waiting to harvest all at once, pick often, as the berries ripen, and ideally do so in the morning before the day heats up.

* Harvested fruit should be placed in cold storage as soon as possible.

SPUR BLIGHT

Spur blight is a fungal disease caused by the pathogen *Didymella applanata*. This primarily attacks raspberries and loganberries, blighting the leaves, spurs and branches of the canes and potentially causing severe damage to the plant.

Lifecycle and Signs of Infection

Spur blights usually infects a plant during late spring to summer, especially in wet conditions. The first signs of spur blight include the development of banded dark brown, blue or purple spots at the base of the leaves' petioles, spreading to the cane. Over time these infected areas will grow and girdle the cane, drying the bark and cracking and splitting the cane.

In the dead wood, around late summer, black speck-like fruiting fungal bodies (pycnidia) will grow. In autumn, the afffected bark will turn silver-gray, with larger black fruiting pustules (perithecia) developing. Fruit on these canes will often shrivel up and die, and those that survive will be small and seedy. New surviving shoots will be stunted and weak.

Leaves on infected canes will turn yellow and drop off, sometimes leaving their stems (petioles) on the cane. Sometimes leaves themselves become infected, developing brown wedge-shaped patches.

Spur blight spores are released in spring and summer, and are carried by the wind or splashed up from the ground onto new canes.

Organic Control Methods

* Spur blight can be controlled with an appropriate fungicide. Infected canes should be removed and destroyed if fruiting bodies are present.

* Since the spur blight spores are spread in wet, warm conditions, improving air circulation around the plant is important to ensure that after rain, the plant does not stay wet for long. This can involve thinning the canes. Keeping the area clear of weeds will also allow for better air flow.

* Some cultivars of raspberry have less susceptibility to spur blight than others. Brandywine, Latham, Newburgh and Killarney are relatively resistant, while others (such as Royalty, Sentry and Willamette) are more easily infected.

* Be careful when doing anything that involves cutting the plant (such as pruning) as the spores enter plant wounds more easily, especially when water makes contact with the sap.

*Avoid watering your plants for 4-5 days after pruning to give them time to heal. Give the plants time to heal after pruning to before watering (4-5 days should be sufficient).

* Treat spur blight as for raspberry cane spot.

BLUEBERRY LEAF RUST

Blueberries are susceptible to fungal leaf diseases when humidity and rainfall are high. In particular, they may be affected by blueberry leaf rust, which is caused by *Pucciniastrum vaccinii*.

Signs of Infection

By the middle of the season, yellow spots appear on leaves. Eventually these turn reddish-brown. On the underside of the leaf, yellowish-orange spore pustules appear. As they age they may turn rusty red.

Organic Control Methods

Fungicide sprays: Protect against leaf rust by applying an organic fungicide. We recommend copper hydroxide (brand names include 'Kocide').In dry climates you can spray with Mancozeb fungicides. Do not wait for leaf damage to appear before spraying. Prevention is better than cure.

Sanitation: Keeping your blueberry bushes clean and healthy is one of the best ways to ensure good control of diseases and pests. Weedy, overgrown garden beds provide shelter and overwintering sites for some pests, so keep your garden tidy.
Infected bushes that are dead or dying can become breeding grounds for other fungi, as well as putting healthy bushes at risk of infection.

Healthy plants: Cultivate your soil regularly. This will kill insects that pupate under dead leaves or near the soil surface. Keep your plants in top condition with a good program of fertilization and irrigation. Healthy plants are better able to tolerate injury from diseases and pests.

Choice of cultivar: Some varieties are more resistant to rust.

MILDEW

Signs of Infection

Mildew can affect blackcurrant bushes. It shows up as a white or grayish powder which can appear on the fruit, leaves and in severe cases on the stem. It probably won't kill the bush, but it will weaken it and make it more susceptible to other diseases.

Powdery mildew
Powdery mildew resembles a white powder which first appears in spring on young emerging leaves. It is similar to a fine coating of talcum powder. If left unchecked it will affect more and more leaves, sometimes also affecting fruit and young twigs.
Infection becomes apparent in spring, though the lifecycle begins in the previous season.

Downy mildew
There is a difference between powdery mildew and downy mildew. Powdery mildew is far more common than downy mildew, but it is vital to recognize the difference between the two so that you can treat them correctly.
Powdery mildew looks like a white powder on both the underside and top of the leaves.
Downy mildew, on the other hand, shows up as a white powder on the underside of the leaves only.

Organic Control Methods

Sprays: You can buy organic sprays to help destroy mildew, although prevention is far better than cure.

Choice of cultivars: Be aware that older varieties of blackcurrants are far more susceptible to mildew. 'Titania' and the 'Ben' cultivars (with the exception of Ben Lomond) of blackcurrants all have some resistance to mildew.

Pruning: The right pruning methods can also reduce the risk of mildew. Be careful to make sure the center of the bush is free from overcrowded branches. Prune bushes when they are dormant. Aims of pruning blackcurrants are:
- To keep the plant pruned back within the available space
- To remove any weak branches and cut off any branches that are touching each other. When they rub together they can wound the bark and allow infection to enter.
- To encourage new growth.
- To keep the center of the bush relatively 'open', thus allowing air circulation. This helps avoid fungal diseases.

CURRANT LEAF SPOT

Currant leaf spot is a fungal disease caused by the organism *Septoria ribis*. It can be identified by the presence of brown, pale-centerd spots on the leaves.

Signs of Infection

Seriously damaged leaves will drop to the ground. If the disease is unchecked, premature defoliation will spread and the tree will be weakened.

Organic control methods

Fallen leaves should be raked and burned to prevent the spread and splashback of the fungal spores.

CATERPILLARS

Check your berry plants for caterpillar damage on a regular basis and control when required. See the the chapter 'General Fruit Pests and Diseases'.

SCALE

Monitor your berry plants for scale insects. The first warning is ant activity, because ants often foster scales. To control scale, pour a small amount of soapy water onto the infested area of the plant. See also the chapter 'General Fruit Pests and Diseases'.

BIRDS AND FLYING FOXES

To prevent raids from birds and flying foxes, cover your berry plants with netting as soon as young fruits appear. See also the 'General Fruit Pests and Diseases' chapter.

6
CACTUS FRUIT

CACTUS FRUIT

Many types of cactus bear delicious fruit. They include:

* The Blueberry Cactus (*Myrtillocactus geometrizans*), also called the Bilberry Cactus, Whortleberry Cactus or Blue Candle, is a cactus species native to central and northern Mexico.

* The Peruvian Apple Cactus (*Cereus repandus*), is a large, erect, thorny columnar cactus native to South America.

* The Indian Fig (Opuntia ficus-indica) is also known as Barbary Fig, Cactus Pear and Spineless Cactus. Not to be confused with its weedy and invasive cousins, Indian Fig is permitted to be cultivated in the cooler southern regions of Australia.

* Dragonfruit, also known as 'sweet pitayas', come in three types, all with leathery, slightly leafy skin:

- White-fleshed Pitaya or Pitaya blanca (*Hylocereus undatus*) has red-skinned fruit with white flesh. This is the most commonly seen 'dragon fruit'.

- Red-fleshed Pitaya or Pitaya roja (*Hylocereus costaricensis*, also known as *Hylocereus polyrhizus*) has red-skinned fruit with red flesh.

- Yellow Pitaya or Pitaya amarilla (*Hylocereus megalanthus* also known as *Selenicereus megalanthus*) has yellow-skinned fruit with white flesh.

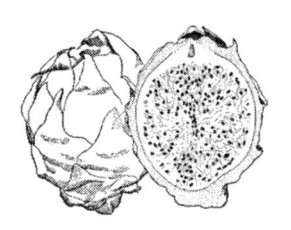

BACTERIAL STEM ROT

Stem rot is an issue with dragonfruit plants. It is caused by a variation of the Xanthomonas campestris bacterium, a pathogen associated with many plant diseases, including fruit, vegetable and tree species. Stem rot, also known as black rot, turns the affected plant tissue a dark brown or black. The bacteria are spread mainly via insect pests such as mites and aphids.

Signs of Infection

Dragon fruit's long stems make it particularly susceptible to a variety of stem rot diseases. Once the stem base becomes infected, the rest of the stem quickly follow suit; the infection then spreads to the leaves, flowers and fruit. Infected plants are at higher risk of environmental damage such as excessive heat or drought. Dragonfruit is considered an ornamental plant; stem rot ruins its aesthetic value by creating unsightly brown and yellow discolorations.

Organic control methods

Critical to the prevention of bacterial stem rot is frequent inspection of the dragon fruit plant to ensure it is growing in a healthy environment. Avoid heavy soils that are easily saturated; these increase the likelihood of stem rot infection in dragon fruit. Similarly, a particularly moist environment may encourage the growth of various strains of fungus that can weaken the plant by damaging its root system.

If you discover signs of stem rot in your dragon fruit plant, it is essential that you remove all the infected stems immediately. Clear away any plant debris to prevent the infection from persisting in rotting tissue beneath the plant.

FUNGAL STEM ROT

The Fusarium oxysporium fungus is another pathogen that causes many diseases of shrubs, plants and trees, dragon fruit included.

Signs of Infection

Fungal stem rot causes infected tissue to become lightly discolored and the stems to lose their integrity. As decay destroys the fibrous tissue in the stems, they will eventually break off.

Organic control methods

Prevention is definitely the best control for fungal stem rot. Make sure your plant is disease-free; avoid plants lacking normal green coloration, have a wilted appearance, or show discoloration in the roots.

Like bacterial stem rot, F. oxysporium is most likely to strike plants that are excessively watered or poorly drained. In the same way, heavy soil lacking good internal drainage makes plants more susceptible to fungal stem rot.

Do not set a new plant any deeper than the soil level in its container. If root rot is already well-established, you may have to replant with a disease-free plant.

Choose cultivars that are known to be resistant to fungal root rot. Keep in mind that even with resistant cultivars, planting in poorly drained soil may result in re-infection. Organic fungicides can be effective in halting fungal root rot's spread if the infection is not too far advanced.

7
CITRUS FRUITS

CITRUS FRUITS

Citrus are high performing but delicate trees, susceptible to many pests, diseases and nutritional deficiencies. In order to get the best out of them, they need careful tending.

Some general tips on maintaining citruses at optimal health: Citrus have shallow roots and feed from soil near the surface. Prevent other plants from competing with them for nutrients by keeping the ground near the base of the tree free from weeds and grass. Apply a thick layer of mulch (lucerne or sugar-cane).

Do not let chickens scratch around the base of citrus trees. Chickens are good at aerating soil and controlling insect pests, but their scratching can damage shallow citrus roots.

Open the citrus plant to better air circulation and sunlight by removing old growth, thickly interlaced twigs and dead wood.

These days there are strong and vigorous citrus rootstocks on the market. Rather than buying from a nursery, some gardeners prefer to contact a specialist supplier who can match the best cultivar with the right root stock for their garden's soil and conditions.

One of the best known citrus pests is fruit fly, which ruins citrus fruit. To control this, purchase an organic fruit fly control from your local nursery or online. See also 'Queensland fruit fly' in the chapter 'General Fruit Pests and Diseases'.

Helpful hint: Mandarins should be picked as soon as they are ripe. If they remain hanging on the tree for too long, they become dry and puffy.

BLACK SPOT

Black spot is a fungal disease endemic to coastal environments.

Signs of Infection

Black spots appears on mature citruses during wet, warm conditions. Valencia oranges are particularly susceptible to infection.

Organic control methods

Spray trees twice with an organic fungicide - the first time at petal-fall, the second 16 weeks afterwards. See our section on organic fungicides.
Harvest oranges as soon as they become ripe, because black spot only attacks mature fruit.

BLOSSOM DROP

Citrus trees naturally shed up to 98% of their blossoms. Usually this is because the tree will bear far too many blossoms to ever develop into fruit.

However, sometimes a citrus tree will only a few blossoms that either fall unopened or shed their petals, leading to a complete crop failure. There are several possible environmental causes for this behaviour – excessive wind or heat, nutritional deficiencies in the soil, a late frost during the blooming period; or lack of (or excess) watering.

Some citruses (such as mandarins, and some oranges and grapefruit) naturally bloom heavily every second year, with the alternate years being a 'light' period (this is known as 'alternate bearing).

Organic control methods

Make sure your citrus' soil is kept irrigated, but is not over-watered. Protecting the tree (if possible) from wind and excessive sun can also help the flowers stay on the tree.

Ensure the tree is well-fertilized. Manure, potash, iron chelates and citrus food are all fertilizers that can be added to improve the soil. Ideally the citrus should be 'fed' three times a year according to the formula of 125g multiplied by the tree's age in years.

BROWN SOFT SCALE

Brown soft scale, Coccus hesperidum, is a citrus scale insect that lays its eggs on citrus trees during the summer. These hatch very quickly and the larva begin to feed on the tree. They molt and reach maturity on twigs or leaves. On rare occasions, they proceed to the fruit.
C. hesperidum populations are most plentiful from the middle of summer through early autumn.

Signs of Infestation

Soft brown scale infestations adversely affect tree vigor, damages shoots and twigs, and reduces fruit yield. The insects excrete honeydew, causing sooty mold to grow and attracting ants, which in turn undermine biological controls of many garden pests.

Organic Control Methods

Natural predators: To control soft brown scales, preserve their natural enemies. The Metaphycus spp. family of parasites is known to attack brown soft scale. Several species of lady beetles also prey on the insect. Avoiding the use of carbamates and organophosphates is vital in retaining scales' natural enemies.

Cut down on ant populations: Reducing the ant population attracted by the scales' honeydew excretions is important in keeping brown soft scale under control.

Oil spray: If this is not sufficient, apply a spot treatment with a spray of horticultural oil.

BROWN SPOT

Citrus Brown Spot may be caused by either fungal or bacterial agents.

Brown Spot (Fungal)

Citrus Brown Spot (which may affect rough lemons, limes and tangerines) is caused by the fungus Alternaria alternata. The fungus spreads from the ground to the tree during wet conditions, attacking the undersides of fruit, leaves and twigs.

Signs of Infection

Affected leaves and fruit will display round-to-oval brown lesions, often surrounded by yellow 'halos'. On the leaves, the lesions are visible on both sides. The fruit lesions, as they age, may turn pale brown and corky, pitting the fruit.

Organic Control Methods

Pruning the lower branches of the tree will lift the leaves and lemons off the ground, making it more difficult for the fungus to spread
It will usually be also necessary to prune the infected twigs, fruit and leaves off the branches of the tree, to remove the infection. Make sure you dispose of them somewhere away from any citrus plants.

Brown Spot (Bacterial)

Brown spots on fruit-fly infested plants may also be caused by bacteria infecting the tiny holes that the fruit-flies puncture in the skin of the fruit.

Organic Control Methods

Get rid of fruit flies using the methods outlined in the chapter 'General Fruit Pests and Diseases'.

CITRUS CANKER

Citrus canker is caused by a bacterium known as Xanthomonas axonopodisa. This is a highly infectious pathogen that thrives in warm and moist environments. X. axonopodisa carried through the air. It is also spread by birds, insects, and human clothing and garden tools. It attacks citrus plants both through cuts in the tree and through natural openings (stomata).

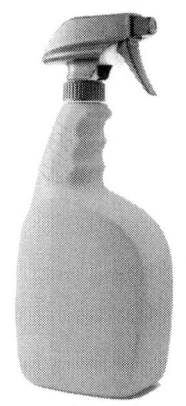

Signs of Infection

Citrus canker causes yellowing and scabs on the leaves and fruit of citrus trees. When the infection is at its worst, it can result in fruit blemishing, early drop, and severe leaf loss.

Citrus canker can be devastating to a country's citrus fruit industry. In the home garden, it means less attractive, usable fruit. Most of the infected fruit tend to prematurely drop from the tree.

Any and all tissues of citrus trees aboveground can be damaged by canker infection. On the leaves and fruit, small lesions will appear, and expand as the tree ages. The hallmark of a canker infection is a yellow 'halo' surrounding the lesions on the leaves. At its center, the leaf will become raised and take on a 'corky' appearance. A very severe infection can completely defoliate the tree.

Organic Control Methods

Prevention is not only better than cure; prevention is the only way to go. Citrus canker is presently incurable. We must manage the disease as carefully as possible so as not to cause cross-contamination.

One of the most effective prevention methods the well-timed application of copper-containing sprays to prevent the disease from becoming airborne and spreading to other trees. Apply these during late summer.

CITRUS COLLAR ROT

Phytophthora citrophthora, citrus collar rot, is a fungal disease that strikes the upper rootsystem of a citrus tree just above the soil level.

Signs of Infection

A tree afflicted by citrus collar rot will have a section of bark surrounding the base of the tree that dies back and eventually detaches itself from the main trunk. Occasionally the necrotic section will crack and ooze gum. There is pronounced yellowing of the leaves, and left unchecked, the disease can result in tree loss.

Organic Control Methods

Cut the bark all the way to the healthy growth and spray the foliage with an organic antifungal. With bark rot, it may be even more effective to make a paste of the antifungal and apply it directly to the affected bark.

Keep mulch and soil well away from the point of the grafting union. Improve oxygen flow by removing mulch touching the tree bark, and ensure proper drainage of the soil around the tree.

CITRUS GALL WASP

This well-known native Australian insect pest, is becoming more and more prevalent. It originated on the East coast in NSW, but has now spread to parts of Victoria and Melbourne. Grapefruit trees have a particular vulnerability to citrus gall wasps, it can also be a problem for limes, lemons and oranges. Rarely, mandarins may be affected.

Signs of Infestation

Citrus gall wasps are tiny, and rarely visible, but lumpy stems and twigs are the best indication that your citrus tree is infested with this pest.
The damage citrus gall wasp infestations cause is mostly aesthetic, although severe cases can weaken the tree, resulting in production loss and dieback.
As the citrus gall larvae burrow into the stems for nutrients, lumpy galls begin to form on branches and trunks. The larvae hatch from just beneath the bark's surface, mainly during spring growth. They then burrow deeper into the bark; this is what triggers the swelling of galls on the twigs. Each gall can provide shelter and food for hundreds of insects.

While galls will not kill the tree, large numbers will weaken the tree, depriving it of nutrients, causing branch dieback and decreasing its fruit crop.

Organic Control Methods

The best way of controlling gall midge wasps is to cut off the galls before the adult insect emerges (in early spring).

Place the refuse in a sealed bag well away from your garden and dispose of it as soon as possible. This will greatly reduce any future infestations.

Warning!
Some nurseries and hardware stores sell bright yellow plastic 'gall wasp traps' (which are also useful for trapping fruit flies). These are coated with a highly adhesive non-drying glue.

Beware: these traps can be highly dangerous to birds! Should even a single feather brush against them the bird becomes stuck fast. Its struggles to free itself only serve to glue more feathers even more firmly. This entrapped, birds cannot fly. They die slowly and in great distress, struggling in pain until their last breath. The worst and most dangerous of these traps are the long, cylindrical-shaped ones.

To protect your useful garden birds from this dreadful fate, either avoid wasp traps altogether, or place the wasp traps inside wire cages, or only buy bird-friendly traps that are manufactured with square mesh already surrounding them. These traps are usually flat and rectangular in shape.

Keep your citrus tree well-nourished with organic manures and composts. Weed the lawn surrounding the tree and water the ground thoroughly. Regular, thorough watering is essential to the health of citrus trees and the production of good fruit. Surround the base of the tree between the trunk and the leaf drip line with organic mulch and/or compost to keep the soil moist and the weeds at bay.

CITRUS LEAFMINER

The citrus leafminer is a serious insect threat to citrus trees. It is a light-colored moth, less than five millimetres long. Its chief identifiers are its silvery and iridescent forewings; these have white and brown markings and a distinctive black spot on the tips of its wings.

While other mining pests affect ornamentals and crop plants, the citrus leafminer is the only insect of this type that attacks citrus leaves specifically.

Phyllocnistis citrella first became a serious pest in Australia in the 1940s; in the 1970s, it appeared in most of the world's other major citrus growing centers.

In its larval stage, leafminer is found on the inside of citrus leaves and the closely-related plants mentioned above. As it grows, the larvae leave a feces trail that appears as a thin, dark line on the underside of the young leaf. This trail is the surest way to identify a leafminer infestation.

Signs of Infestation

The leafminer larvae feed by creating small tunnels (mines) in the young leaves of lemon, lime, grapefruit, orange, and mandarin trees, causing them to curl inward and distort. They may also strike closely related plants, such as calamondin and kumquat. At the end of its larval stage, the insect comes out of the mine and moves toward the leaf's edge. It uses the leaf as a protective covering while it pupates.

Young citrus trees are particularly susceptible to leafminer infestation. The insect can stunt tree growth and cause a reduced fruit yield. Large leafminer populations are often fatal to young trees. The insect is a particular problem in cool coastal areas.

The inital growth of citrus trees under attack by the leafminer are unsightly, prompting growers to take action early. Still, the best strategy may not involve insecticides at all; rather, allow the citrus leafminer's natural enemies to parasitize the larvae while they are in their mines. In Australia, where leafminer infestation is long-established, serious damage to citrus trees in their first few years of life is often followed by reduced severity due to the feeding of these natural enemies. These parasites seek out mining insects and lay their eggs inside them. Leafminer populations tend to decline as these parasite populations grow.

Organic control methods

Pheromone traps are a highly effective way of determining citrus leafminer populations. These traps are baited with a natural chemical insect sex attractant (pheremone); while they are useful for detection, they are usually not able to catch enough of the insects to be useful for population control. This is partly due to the fact that only the male moths are attracted to the pheromone. When using traps, it is important to identify the trapped moths before taking other action; they should be checked weekly for several weeks.

Wasps are an important ally in controlling leafminer populations. Very small wasps, such as the Pnigalio species, lay their eggs inside the mine; when the eggs hatch, the wasp larva consume the leafminer larva from within. One reason to resist using chemical insecticides is that they often kill these natural enemies of the leafminer as well.

Prune live branches no more than once a year, allowing for uniform, brief flushing cycles. If the leaves are left to harden, the pests will be unable to bore into the leaves. Unaffected leaves will continue to produce nutrients for the tree; you do not need to prune off mildly affected leaves.

That said, curled or rolled leaves should be removed, since they might be hiding and protecting pupae.

The leafminer can be prevented from laying its eggs by spraying white oil on both sides of the leaves (especially new growth). Spraying should be done three times, at three-week intervals.

A home-made oil-spray can be made by mixing a teaspoon of liquid detergent with a cup of vegetable oil and diluting the mixture with water according to the ratio 1:40.

Nitrogen fertilizer is not recommended if you are trying to control this pest. Nitrogen triggers fast, lush, weak and soft growth. 'Water sprouts' often develop on branches and, grow rapidly, producing new leaves for quite some time. If citrus leafminer infestation is a problem, remove these fast-growing shoots. They may provide an ideal place for moths to lay their eggs. Water sprouts do not usually produce desirable fruit.

CITRUS THRIPS

Citrus thrips, or Scirtothrips citri, are very small yellow or orange insects that attack citrus and other fruiting trees. As with the whitefly, the damage is done by larvae feeding on the young leaves. Both the damage done and the control method recommended are identical to those of citrus whitefly.

CITRUS WHITEFLY

The citrus whitefly (Dialeurodes citri) is a white, winged insect that feeds on the underside of citrus tree leaves and that lays its eggs in the same place.

Signs of Infestation

The juvenile whiteflies immediately begin sucking the sap from the leaves. As the leaves are sucked dry of nutrients, they curl inward and become covered with a sticky substance not unlike sooty mold.

Organic control methods

If you find evidence of a whitefly infestation, spray your citrus trees with an organic pesticide. Once an adult whitefly population is established, it becomes nearly impossible to wipe out. Your best bet is to spray your trees several times to put a serious dent in the juvenile population.

SOFT BROWN ROT

Soft brown rot is another fungus that develops on fallen fruit. In wet conditions, the spores are splashed back onto the tree, infecting living fruit.

Signs of Infection

Brown, soft and stinking spots appear on the fruit skin.

Organic Control Methods

Remove all fallen fruit from the ground. If any are clear of rot they can be eaten, but the rest must be disposed of far from the tree. Prune the lower branches of the tree up to one metre above the ground. Apply mulch around the base of the tree.

SOOTY MOLD

Signs of Infection

Sooty mold (Capnodium mangiferae) is a fungal infection that appears as a black, sticky substance on citrus tree leaves, stems and twigs. The mold itself does not feed on the plant, but because it covers the leaf surface, it blocks out sunlight, thus reducing vital photosynthesis. In effect, it starves the plant of the light it needs to grow.

Organic Control Methods

Usually, sooty mold is a result of an infestation of insects that secrete honeydew. These insects include aphids, scale, mealybugs and white flies. Controlling the insects will remove the source of the honeydew, after which the sooty mold, deprived of its food, will dry up.

The black substance will eventually fall or wash off the foliage. To control insect populations, apply 100% organic insecticide or white oil over the leaves of your citrus tree.

SPINED CITRUS BUGS AND BRONZE-ORANGE BUGS

Spined citrus/bronze-orange bugs are flat bugs around the size of a fingernail or larger. They feed on the many varieties of citrus fruits.

Spined citrus bugs have 'horn-like' spines on the sides of their heads and may be yellow, orange or green in color.

Bronze-orange bugs are brown and orange in color, and exude an acrid 'stink' when disturbed.

Signs of Infestation

These bugs cause dimpling and gumming on the fruit skin, and significantly damage the inside - drying and browning the fruit segments, rendering them inedible. Often the damaged fruit falls prematurely.

Organic Control Methods

Spray the tree with horticultural oil, during the cooler months.

Spined citrus bug

MELANOSE

Signs of Infection

Melanose (*Mycosphaerella citri* and *Diaporthe citri*) occurs in coastal areas and produces dark brown spots (or 'tear stains') on the fruit, leaves and twigs.

Organic control methods

Infection is reduced by spraying with protectant copper fungicides after petals fall. See our section on organic fungicides.

NUTRIENT DEFICIENCIES

It is common for gardeners to underestimate the amount of nutrients required by a citrus tree. This results in nutritional deficiencies.

A tree's ability to absorb certain nutrients is also affected by the soil pH. The ideal pH for citrus soil is between 5.5 and 6.5. When fertilizing citrus the pH of the soil should be monitored.

Since nutrients are 'leached' out of the soil in wet or sandy conditions, this should also be taken into consideration when feeding the plant, since different conditions may cause it require even more nutrients than normal.

Symptoms of nitrogen imbalance

Nitrogen deficiency in citruses causes yellowing leaves, twig dieback, small fruit and stunted shoots. Conversely excess nitrogen causes thick-skinned fruit with possible 'regreening'.

Symptoms of phosphorus imbalance

Phosphorus deficiency in citrus trees is signified by bronzing of the leaves, thickening of the skin and distortion of the fruit shape. Excess of phosphorus causes thinner peel, greater juice and acidity.

Symptoms of iron deficiency

Iron deficiency in citruses is indicated by chlorotic (pale) leaves with darker green veins, stunted growth and reduced fruit yield.

Symptoms of potassium imbalance

Deficiencies in potassium typically lead to leaf, flower and fruit-drop, diminished leaf size and small thin-skinned fruit that are prone to splitting. Too much potassium leads to delayed fruit maturity and the formation of rough, thick rinds.

Symptoms of magnesium deficiency

Magnesium-deficient citruses will display yellowing at the apex of the leaves, until in advanced cases only a small green triangle remains at the base of the leaf. In severe cases the tree will suffer shoot dieback and defoliation. Fruit will be small and yield low.

Symptoms of zinc deficiency

When citrus trees become zinc-deficient their leaves display a pattern of white-to-yellow blotches, the leaves themselves become narrower, tree growth becomes stunted, and the plant may experience twig dieback.

Symptoms of copper imbalance

Symptoms of copper deficiency in citrus include shoot dieback, brown peel and the presence of brown gum patches on young shoots and fruit. The presence of too much copper will cause stunted roots and retarded growth.

Symptoms of manganese imbalance

A deficiency of manganese will cause the plant's young leaves to turn mottled green, with yellowing between the leaf veins. This is accompanied by a slight decrease in growth and yield. Excessive quantities of manganese is toxic to the plant, and the citrus will exhibit bright yellowing on the edges of the leaves, which will be accompanied by dark brown 'tar spots'.

Solutions to Nutritional Imbalance

- Iron deficiency can be treated with iron chelates, applied twice a year in autumn and spring. For small trees, poultry manure can be sprinkled around the base of the plant, and 'watered in' with a solution of two teaspoons of iron chelates to four and a half litres of water.
- Magnesium deficiency can be solved by sprinkling Epsom salts around the base of the plant and watering in.
- Every spring, water your trees with trace elements.
- Four times a year, every season, apply certified organic poultry manure at a rate of one handful per square metre. This will address nitrogen deficiency.
- Every fortnight, feed your trees using either seaweed or a flower and fruit fertilizer.
- Don't feed citrus while they're in flower. If you do, you'll get lots of beautiful leaves, but very few fruit.
- A good all-purpose fertilizer can be made from three tablespoons of seaweed concentrate, one teaspoon of trace elements and two teaspoons of iron chelates mixed with 4.5 litres of water.
- Citrus can be 'sweetened' by sprinkling six handfuls of potash around the base of the tree and watering it in with a mixture of two teaspoons Epsom salts to ten litres of water.

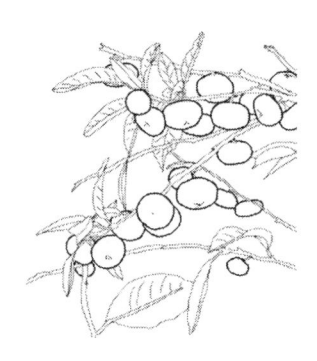

8

FIGS

Figs are generally hardy plants, with fewer problems than more delicate fruits such as citrus or cherry.

This does not however mean that they are not prone to some pests and diseases.

ANTHRACNOSE

Anthracnose is a fungus that attacks a variety of fruit growing in coastal areas, including figs and avocados. It is described in more detail in the 'General Fruit Pests and Diseases' chapter.

The sweetness and softness of figs make them particularly susceptible to birds. How to prevent these feathery pests from stealing your fruit crop is covered in greater detail in the 'General Fruit Pests and Diseases' chapter.

DRIED FRUIT BEETLE

The dried fruit beetle (Carpophilus spp.) is a small, dark brown beetle with short wing covers and (sometimes) yellow markings. They attack a range of fruit, including stonefruit and citrus. In fact, having planting figs near these other fruit trees makes Carpophilus infestation more likely.

Signs of Infestation

Ironically, the 'dried fruit beetle' tends to avoid mature, drying figs – targeting instead the developing fruit. It enters through the eye and feeds as either a larva or an adult. This causes damage to the fruit, and if the beetle is an adult, it will also carry yeast into the fruit, which causes souring.

Organic Control Methods

The most effective organic for this pest is prevention. Since the beetles winter in the fallen fruits of previously infested trees (such as citruses), rigorous removal of fallen fruit from the ground over winter will prevent the beetles taking hold in your figs next season.

FIG BLISTER MITE

The fig blister mite (Aceria ficus) is a tiny, white or colorless insect that feeds on mainly unripe (but sometimes ripe) fruit.

Signs of Infestation

The presence of fig blister mite cannot be detected from the exterior of the fruit since the insect enters the plant and feeds on the florets near the opening. The damage (rusty dry patches) is only apparent when the fruit is cut. While the fig blister mite does not cause serious damage on its own, the eating quality of individually affected fruit is reduced, and there is a risk that the mites may spread the fig mosaic virus to your plants.

Organic Control Methods

It is difficult to control the fig blister mite since the fruit needs to be cut to be detected. Fortunately the first ripe fruits of the season are most likely to be infested, so sampling a selection of these early fruit, and discarding them if they are damaged, can help prevent the rest of the crop from being affected.

FIG MOSAIC VIRUS

This virus affects the pigment of the leaves, causing a distinctive mottled 'mosaic' pattern. It is spread by the fig blister mite, or when people graft or take cuttings from already infected trees.

Signs of Infection

By destroying the pigment in the leaves, the virus reduces the plant's ability to photosynthesise. This stunts growth and fruit production diminishes.

Organic Control Methods

The fig mosaic virus is incurable – as a result, if you have an affected plant near any healthy figs, you should remove your infected plant immediately, and check the healthy plants for presence of the fig blister mite, which may be spreading the disease. Practice orchard hygiene, pruning healthy trees before infected ones. Never use a virus-infected plant for propagation or grafting. Clean your pruning tools with bleach or mrthylated spirits.

FIG RUST

Fig rust is caused by a fungus. It chiefly attacks figs growing in humid coastal areas.

Signs of Infection

The fungal disease can be identified by the presence of powdery yellow spots on the fig leaves, which if left uncontrolled will turn the whole leaf yellow, causing it to fall off. A bad case of fig rust will seriously defoliate a tree.

Organic Control Methods

As with the other fungal diseases, fig rust responds well to copper-based fungicides.

FIG FRUIT DROP

Fig fruit drop may be due to a range of factors, ranging from inclement or unseasonably cool weather, lack of water or sunlight, lack of pollination, nutrient deficiencies or nematodes.

QUEENSLAND FRUIT FLY

Strategies for preventing and dealing fruit fly are outlined in detail in the 'General Fruit Pests and Diseases' chapter.

ROOT-KNOT NEMATODE

Root-knot nematodes (*Meloidogyne spp.*) are tiny pests that damage plants by creating galls ('knots') in the roots, restricting the plant's ability to take up water and nutrients from the soil. They are more likely to become a problem when the tree is newly-planted, or when the soil is sandy.

Signs of Infection

Damaged trees become stunted and turn yellow. Trees with seriously damaged roots may die. Lesion, root knot, and dagger nematodes can reduce growth and fruit yield. Infested trees are more likely to be susceptible to temperature and water stress.

Organic Control Methods

The soil can be 'biofumigated' for the fig tree if a green manure crop of mustard is planted in the site beforehand then slashed, covered with soil and allowed to decompose naturally.
It is possible to graft a nematode-resistant fig variety to a non-resistant rootstock, giving some protection from the pests.
See the chapter on 'General Fruit Pests and Diseases'.

9

GRAPES

GRAPE PHYLLOXERA

Grape phylloxera (*Daktulosphaira vitifolii*) is a small aphid-like insect that is barely visible to the naked eye. In the southern hemisphere the species generally attacks the grapevine roots although sometimes that also cause leaf-galls. They feed on the roots, which disrupts the plant's ability to take up water and nutrients. This causes debilitation of the vines and usually ends up killing European Vitis vinifera vines.

Rootstocks can provide varying degrees of tolerance to the pest.

Signs of Infestation
Symptoms of phylloxera are very similar to symptoms of moisture stress. They include weak, short shoots, pale leaves and reduced crop yields.

Organic Control Methods
There is no cure for phylloxera; however, the use of phylloxera-tolerant rootstocks may control insect numbers. It is thought that phylloxera moves from vineyard to vineyard on plant material, on machinery and on clothing or equipment of vineyard workers and visitors.

LIGHT BROWN APPLE MOTH

Light brown apple moth (*Epiphyaspostvittana*) is a native Australian moth which is can be damaging to a number of fruit crops. The species tends to die off at high temperatures and is therefore a more serious issue in cooler areas with mild summers.

Signs of Infestation
Light brown apple moths lay their eggs in rafts of 20 to 50, generally on the upper surfaces of leaves or on shoots. The tiny bluish-green eggs turn green-yellow when the larvae are about to hatch. The yellow larvae (caterpillars) become green as they mature.

Caterpillars roll shoots and leaves together into bunches and tie them with silken thread. They feed on these leafy bunches. Look for their chrysalises, which are brown and approximately 1 cm long, and attached to the vine at the feeding site within webby leaves and shoots or bunches.

Large caterpillars can occasionally crawl onto vines at budburst and destroy new buds. Damage to developing and ripening bunches by light brown apple moths can also increase the incidence of Botrytis bunch rot infections, especially in cooler and wetter areas.

Organic Control Methods

Cultural: Remove potential light brown apple moth host plants such as broad-leaved weeds and plant non-host plants such as grasses.

Natural enemies: Numerous natural predators such as lacewings, spiders and predatory shield bugs can keep down the numbers of light brown apple moths.

The most efficient natural enemy of light brown apple moth is *Trichogramma*, a genus of tiny wasps that parasitise and develop in light brown apple moth eggs, thereby destroying the eggs. You can buy these wasps from several companies.

Pheremones: Light brown apple moth can be controlled by mating disruption, through the use of a synthetic pheromone chemically identical to the natural pheromone produced by female moths to attract male moths. When slow-release dispensers containing this pheremone are positioned throughout vineyards, males cannot find females because their natural pheromones are drowned out by the synthetic pheromones. Without mating, the eggs laid by the females are not fertile and no larva will hatch. This interrupts the moths' lifecycle.

Organic pesticides: As a last resort you could try using an insecticide registered for light brown apple moths. There are several new insecticides on the market that are 'milder'. These are specific to caterpillar pests and have a minimal effect on non-target species.

The insecticides work best if you spray them after the eggs have hatched, and before caterpillars reach 3 to 5 mm in length and start to roll up leaves and build silken feeding shelters.

Caterpillars hiding inside leaf bunches are hard to control. Biological insecticides containing the bacterium *Bacillus thuringiensis* (Bt) specifically kill only caterpillars and not their natural enemies. The caterpillars have to actually eat the Bt insecticides for it to work.

GRAPEVINE MOTH

Grapevine moth (*Phalaenoides glycinae*) is usually a minor pest, but if the caterpillar population gets too high, they can cause severe vine defoliation. This in turn affects the development and flavour of the grapes.

Signs of Infestation

Leaves will appear chewed. You may see the adult moths - they are black with white and yellow markings, a wingspan of about 6 cm, and tufts of orange hair on the tip of the abdomen and around the legs. Moths fly about during the day in groups, feeding on nectar and pollen.

Early in spring the moths emerge from the pupae where they have spent the winter. They immediately lay eggs on stems and leaves. The spherical eggs are round, sculptured and green to brown in colour.

Also look for caterpillars, which are chiefly black and white with red markings, coated in scattered white hairs. They can grow up to 5 cm in length.

Caterpillars feed on leaves but may begin feeding in bunches of fruit if there are not enough leaves.

Organic control methods

Parasitoids such as tachinid flies and wasps, predatory shield bugs and birds offer some control against the pest.
Several organic insecticides are registered for grapevine moth. See the chapter on 'Pest and Disease Remedies'

GRAPEVINE HAWK MOTH AND VINE HAWK MOTH

Grapevine hawk moth is *Hippotion celerio* and Vine hawk moth is *Theretra oldenlandiae*.
Mature hawk moth caterpillars grow to a similar size as the grapevine moth (up to 5 cm in length). They have a fleshy spine on the upper rear end of the body, and brightly coloured eye spots along the body.
Adult moths fly only at night. They have wingspans of about 7 cm, are largely grey or brown coloured, and are expert fliers that are often attracted to lights.

Organic Control Methods

These are not a frequent pest of grapes, but if you need to control them, use a registered organic pesticide such as the bacterium *Bacillus thuringiensis*.

Male Vine Hawk Moth

VINE BORER MOTH

The vine borer moth is a member of the *Echiomima* genus.

Signs of Infestation
Adult moths are approximately 10 -15 mm long and creamy white to light brown in color. They have a thick tuft of white hair under their heads, and frequently display a black dot on each forewing.

The moths fly at nights, usually in early- to mid-summer. The tiny eggs are white and cylindrical in shape. Moths lay them in bark crevices around the dormant buds on spurs near the cordon. Larvae feed on the surface of the bark or dormant buds before boring their way into the heartwood. They chiefly eat the outer sapwood and bark around the spur and cordon, which effectively ring-barks the spur or cordon, thus destroying it.

Larvae feed beneath a sheltering carpet of larval 'frass' (their own excretions), which they trap in a web of silk. These masses make it easy to spot this pest while you are pruning your vines. Larvae grow to about 25 mm long and as they grow they eat more and cause more damage.

Over a few seasons this continued feeding damagemay lead to loss of vigour, crop losses through loss of fruiting spurs, and dieback.

Organic Control Methods
Parasitoids such as tachinid flies and wasps, predatory shield bugs and birds offer some control against the pest.
A registered organic pesticide such as the bacterium *Bacillus thuringiensis* can be useful.

MEALYBUG

Three species of mealybug (Pseudococcus sp.) are commonly found in vineyards: longtailed mealybug (*Pseudococcus longispinus*), citrophilus mealybug (*Pseudococcus calceolariae*) and obscure mealybug (*Pseudococcus affinis*). Longtailed mealybug is the most serious pest of grapes.

Mealybugs are soft-bodied sucking insects covered in white, hair-like wax. Adult females grow to about 5 mm in length and have no wings. Males are a lot smaller and have wings.

Female mealybugs can lay huge numbers of eggs, which rapidly hatch into crawlers. Mealybugs prefer mild, humid conditions and most of them die off during hot, dry conditions.

Signs of Infestation

Mealybugs do not usually cause huge amounts of damage. If their population grows large, their excretions of sticky honeydew leads to the development of sooty mold on leaves and fruit. When sooty mold coats grape vine leaves it can reduce the plant's photosynthesis. Sooty and mold on grapes can make the fruit unsaleable, or lead to rotting.

Organic Control Methods

Longtailed mealybug has several natural enemies including predatory ladybeetle beetles and lacewings, and parasitic wasps. The native Australian ladybeetle species *Cryptolaemus montrouzieri* prefers feeding on mealybugs and you can buy these from companies that sell biological control agents.

Ants may crawl up your grape vines to feed on honeydew. They encourage the proliferation of mealybug colonies by deterring mealybugs' natural enemies.

If you see large numbers of ants, apply sticky trap coatings to the trunk. This will exclude ants from vines.

Organic insecticides may be used to reduce ant numbers but be careful not to kill the beneficial bugs that are so helpful in the garden.

Sprays are rarely required on wine grapes. You should spray only in cases where you know you've lost a fair proportion of your crop in the past, and when you can see that there is a lot of damage from mealybugs. Use a registered organic product if insecticidal control is required.

MITES

Mites are not insects. Unlike insects they have two distinct body segments, no antennae and usually four pairs of legs.

The easiest way to distinguish between various mite pests of grapevines is by the damage that they do. The scientific name *Colomerus vitis* is applied to both bud and blister mites.

GRAPELEAF BUD MITE

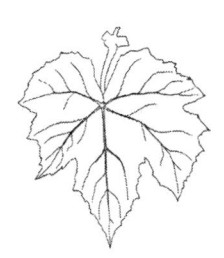

Grapeleaf bud mite (*Colomerus vitis*) is 0.2 mm long, creamy white in colour. It resembles a worm, except that it has two pairs of legs near the head. Up to 12 generations can hatch out in a 12 month period, with later generations in autumn chewing deeper in the developing buds, thus damaging cells which would have become leaves and fruit in the following season.

Signs of Infestation

Feeding by grapeleaf bud mites can cause deformed leaves, aborted or damaged grape bunches and the death of buds.
Keep a close eye on your grapevines. Examine dormant winter buds, looking for the characteristic 'tissue bubbling' damage around the outer scales.

Organic Control Methods
See 'Organic mite control methods', below.

GRAPELEAF BLISTER MITE

Grapeleaf blister mite and bud mite (*Colomerus vitis*), although similar in shape and color, can be distinguished by the damage they cause.

Signs of Infestation

Grapeleaf blister mites feed on leaves. They cause very obvious blisters on the leaves' upper surfaces, and white or brown hairy growths within the raised blisters on the lower surface of leaves. The damage can look bad but fortunately generally it does not reduce crop yield very much.

Organic Control Methods

See 'Organic mite control methods', below.

GRAPELEAF RUST MITE

Grapeleaf rust mites (*Calepitrimerus vitis*) are in the same family (Eriophyidae) as bud and blister mites, and they look similar, but they are more active.

Signs of Infestation

The damage is most obvious in spring, from the moment of leaf-bud burst to the time when five to eight leaves have appeared. The damage then becomes less apparent as the shoots recover and grow out. You can still see serious early spring damage in mature leaves through the growing season.

The most apparent and easily recognisable symptoms of rust mite infestation take place between midsummer and autumn. The leaves begin to darken and take on a bronzed appearance due to rust mites feeding on, and damaging, the surface cells of the leaf.

Organic Control Methods

See 'Organic mite control methods', below.

BUNCH MITE

Bunch mite adults (*Brevipalpus californicus* and *Brevipalpus lewisi*) are 0.3 mm long, flat, shield-shaped and colored reddish-brown.

Signs of Infestation

Early season damage shows up as small dark spots or scars around the base of grapevine canes. They then appear on the fruit bunch stalks, berry pedicels and the grapes themselves. Damage to the bunch stalks and pedicels can partly starve the grapes, preventing them from accumulating sugars and thus affecting sweetness and flavor.

Organic Control Methods

See 'Organic mite control methods', below.

TWO-SPOTTED MITE

Two-spotted mite (*Tetranychus urticae*)

Signs of Infestation

These mites such the sap out of grape vines. This causes cause chlorosis or yellowing of leaves. Severe infestations can cause leaves to die. As they feed they spin a characteristic webbing on the underside of leaves.

Organic Control Methods

Outbreaks of two-spotted mite can almost always be linked to sprayings of insecticides that kill off to their natural enemies. The best strategy for control is to avoid the use of insecticides. See also organic mite control methods below.

ORGANIC MITE CONTROL METHODS

Despite the fact that the general control principles for the control of rust, bud and blister mites are similar, it is recommended that you use different control methods for each species.

* **Natural enemies**. Several predatory insects and spiders feed on mites but the most efficient natural predators of mite pests are predatory mites. Two species, *Euseius victoriensis* ('Victoria') and *Typhlodromus doreenae* ('Doreen'), are especially good at maintaining low pest mite populations.

* **Organic pesticide**: If you really need to use chemicals to control severe infestations of pest mites, use a registered organic pesticide. Read the instructions on the label and apply the pesticide at an appropriate time to provide good control.
The 'good bugs', the predatory mites, are susceptible to several insecticides and fungicides. Therefore it's in your best interests to select chemicals that are friendly to predatory mites to ensure high numbers of predatory mites in the vineyard.

* **Timing**: Control populations of bud mite straight after budburst. This is the time when mites are exposed on bud scales and leaf axils.
Blister mite rarely requires control but, if necessary, spray them at the wooly bud stage.

* **Rust mite treatment**: You can treat rust mite most effectively by spraying large quantities of wettable sulphur and oil. This should be done at the time of chardonnay woolly bud stage and when temperatures reach at least 15°C.

NEMATODES

A number of nematode species attack grapevine roots. They include root knot (*Meloidogyne sp.*), citrus (*Tylenchulus semipenetrans*), root lesion (*Pratylenchus sp.*), ring (*Criconemella sp.*), spiral (*Helicotylenchus sp.*), pin (*Paratylenchus sp.*), dagger (*Xiphinema sp.*), stunt (*Tylenchorhynchus sp.*) and stubby root (*Paratrichodorus sp.*) nematodes.

These parasites all live in soil and feed on root cells. Their feeding interrupts the plant's uptake of nutrients and water from the soil. Root knot, citrus and root lesion nematodes are very common.

Signs of Infestation

The chief symptoms of nematode damage are stunted growth, reduced vigour and yellowing leaves. These symptoms can look a lot like nutrient deficiencies or drought stress. Look closely at the roots. Plant parasitic nematodes commonly cause dark patches or death of the root surface.

Thin and dense fibrous roots are the usual symptoms of stubby root nematodes.

Cells infected with root knot nematode swell into characteristic 'galls' or 'knots' in the roots whereas citrus-nematode-infected cells become thickened and discoloured.

Different plant parasitic nematodes prefer to attack different plants. Root knot and root lesion nematodes can infect many fruiting plants. The citrus nematode can attack not only grapevines but also olives, citrus and pears.

Many nematode species can survive for up to two years in the soil without any host plants.

Organic Control Methods

* **Choose your cultivars**. When planting grapevines, find out if the soil you are about to plant in has recently been used for other fruiting plants. If it has, then there is a slightly higher risk it's infested with nematodes.
Nematode tolerant rootstocks can provide some protection from these pests.

* **Plant nematode-free grapevines** that have been treated with hot water to eliminate any possible introduction of nematodes from nursery to vineyards.

* **Biofumigation**. For established grapevines, biofumigation can be very helpful. Plant Brassicas as a cover crop. Brassica species suppress nematodes through the release of a chemical called isothiocyanate as they break down in the soil.
The mustard cultivar 'Nemfix' is a Brassica. You can buy it from seed suppliers. To really decimate a nematode population, grow the mustard as close as possible to the vines, then when it's at its full height slash it. Let it lie on the ground and cover it with soil.

* **Organic pesticide**: as a last resort use a registered organic pesticide.

BIRDS

Several species of birds can cause severe damage to ripening grapes. Scaring devices and the use of netting provide some control. A chemical repellent is also available. See the chapter 'General Pests and Diseases'.

GRAPEVINE SCALE

Signs of Infestation

Grapevine scale (*Parthenolecanium persicae*) is a tiny, oval-shaped sucking insect that protects itself with a dark brown wax cover. Scales are visible to the naked eye. They can be seen attached mainly to the stems or canes of grapevines, where they feed. Large numbers of these pests can stunt vine growth and reduce crop yield.

The chief issue with grapevine scale is that it excretes honeydew, which drops onto leaves and fruit bunches. This causes the growth of sooty mold, with a resultant decrease in photosynthesis. Consequently the grapevine's growth and productivity will suffer.

Grapevine scale has one annual generation. Immature scales over-winter on the previous season's wood and begin maturing in spring.

During late spring and summer, mature scales deposit hundreds of eggs under their bodies and then die. Crawlers hatch and move to the leaves to feed but later move back to the canes to feed, where they remain during winter.

Organic Control Methods

* **Pruning**: If you carefully prune the grapevine canes you can provide excellent control by cutting off and discarding the wood that carries most of the over-wintering scale population.

* **Natural predators:** Several parasitic wasps and predators such as ladybeetles and lacewings help control of grapevine scale.

* **Ant removal**: Ants that feed on the honeydew can deter these natural enemies so control the ants with sticky traps and horticultural glues.

* **Organic insecticides**: These work best after pruning in winter or early spring when scale are juvenile and there are not as many of them around. It is harder to successfully control scale in summer because it's is more difficult to get a good spray coverage in dense leaf canopies.

Use a registered chemical if insecticidal control is required. See the chapter on 'Pest and Disease Remedies'

FIG LONGICORN BORER

The fig longicorn borer (*Acalolepta vastator*) is a beetle whose newly hatched larvae bore into the grapevine wood and can tunnel throughout the trunk and into roots. This pest can cause serious damage to the vine trunk, which can lead to dieback and significant reductions in crops.

Signs of Infestation

The adult beetle is about 3 cm long and has antennae longer than the body. You can often see larval excrement and sawdust inside the holes bored by the grubs, and around the vine's trunk.

Organic Control Methods

Borers are difficult to control because the boring stage is usually not accessible to insecticides. Carefully prune wood that may contain larvae and discard the prunings by sealing them in plastic and putting them in the bin. See the chapter on 'Pest and Disease Remedies'

ELEPHANT WEEVIL

Signs of Infestation

The adult elephant weevil (*Orthorhinus cylindrirostris*) measures about 8 to 20 mm in length. Its body is thickly covered with scales coloured from grey to black.
Most beetles emerge during early spring, when they lay eggs in holes that they drill at the base of the vine. The larvae burrow inside the wood of the vine, leaving visible holes. they stay inside for about 10 months, then pupate before ermerging as adults.

Organic Control Methods

See the chapter on 'Pest and Disease Remedies'

FRUIT-TREE BORER

The adult moths of the fruit-tree borer (*Maroga melanostigma*) tend to lay their eggs in wound sites on the bark and wood of the grapevine.

Signs of Infestation

Look for small egges clustered in cracks in the bark. The larvae hatch, then feed on the bark before boring into the wood. This leaves evidence of small holes in the graevine's wood and other bark damage. Larvae can also ring-bark limbs and trunks. Large numbers of larvae can cause parts of the vines to die.

Organic Control Methods

See the chapter on 'Pest and Disease Remedies'

PESTS OF YOUNG GRAPEVINES

The major insect pests that tend to attack young grapevines include:
- African black beetle (*Heteronychus arator*)
- Apple weevil (*Otiorhynchus cribricollis*)
- Garden weevil (*Phlyctinus callosus*)
- Cutworms (*Agrotisspp.*)
- Budworms (*Helicoverpaspp.*) These are caterpillar pests that can wreak havoc on newly planted vines by feeding on leaves at night.

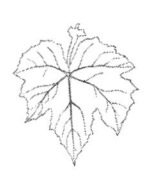

Signs of Infestation

These species chew the bark and ringbark young vines, which weakens the canes and sometimes kills them. Look for these pests during the hours of darkness when they come out to feed.

Organic Control Methods

If your garden has a history of weevils and beetles, spray with a registered organic pesticide before you plant your grapevines. It's harder to get rid of pests after the planting. Spray the organic registered insecticide at night for best control.

See the chapter on 'Pest and Disease Remedies'

10

GUAVAS

Guavas are plants in the Myrtle family genus Psidium, which contains about 100 species of tropical and sub-tropical shrubs and small trees. They are native to Mexico, Central America, and northern South America.
–*Wikipedia*

Guavas commonly grown in home gardens include the Apple Guava (Psidium guajava) and the Peruvian Guava (Psidium cattleianum).

GUAVA ANTHRACNOSE

Mentioned in the 'General Fruit Pests and Diseases' chapter, anthracnose can be a serious disease in guava plants. *Pestalotiopsis psidii, Colletotrichum gloeosporioides* and *Botryodiplodia theobromae* are organisms that cause it. The *P. psidii* pathogen affects all parts of the guava plant except its root system.

Signs of Infection

The tips of infected plants turn a dark brown, with black necrotic tissue extending backwards, causing dieback of the entire plant. The fruit of an infected guava plant will exhibit pinpoint spots, particularly during heavy rains. Eventually, these spots come together to create large lesions. Grey spots will also appear on the tips and margins of the plant's leaves.

Organic Control Methods

- Prune and burn affected twigs.
- Plant Apple Guava, a relatively resistant cultivar.
- See the chapter on 'Pest and Disease Remedies'

FRUIT CANKER

Signs of Infection

Known as the *colletotrichum* fungus, fruit canker infections cause small brown circles of necrotic growth in immature guava fruit. These circles tend to be shallow and appear on the surface of the skin; nevertheless, they impact the aesthetic value of the fruit. Infected fruits lose ascorbic acid rapidly. Canker is most serious during periods of heavy rains.

Organic Control Methods

- Remove infected plant parts immediately upon detection. If possible, plant resistant varieties such as 'Allahabad safeda' and 'Banarasi supreme.'
- Spraying 1% Bordeaux mixture may be an effective means of controlling this disease.

STRIPED MEALY BUG

The striped mealy bug, *Ferrisia virgata*, is a tiny insect that sucks the sap from twigs, leaves and flowers.

Signs of Infestation

Infested fruit will generally be misshapen and of poor quality. An *F. virgata* infestation also renders the fruit more susceptible to secondary infections by a variety of pathogens.

Organic Control Methods

- Band the tree trunk with polyethylene film to prevent the nymphs from climbing up from the soil.
- Spray the fruit with neem oil or liquid soap and plenty of water. Repeat this procedure for ten days or until the infestation is eradicated.

WILT OF GUAVA

Wilt of guava is a fungal disease caused by the *Fusarium solani* pathogen. This disease is most prevalent in rainy periods and in alkaline soil.

Signs of Infection

Plants affected by wilt of guava often exhibit yellowed leaves. The leaves and twigs subsequently begin to dry up and eventually the entire tree wilts.

Organic Control Methods

- Be sure to remove all the dry twigs and uproot the wilted plant.
- Balance the plant's nutrients, with an emphasis on organic sources of nitrogen.
- The Allahabad Safeda and Banarasi Supreme guava cultivars are naturally resistant to wilt of guava.

11

NUTS

Almonds, walnuts, hazelnuts, macadamia, pecans, chestnuts etc. are popular in home gardens. We have included cashews in this section despite the fact that they are actually not nuts at all, but seeds. The tropical evergreen cashew tree is a native of Brazil, although it flourishes in tropical regions aroud the world.

ANTHRACNOSE

For information about anthracnose on nut trees, see 'General Fruit Pests and Diseases'.

BACTERIAL CANKER

Bacterial canker, also known as gummosis, is a widespread disease that can affect many fruit and nut tree hosts; particularly almonds.

Signs of Infection

Bacterial canker enters the tree through the wounds caused by damage to bark or leaves. Infected trees may be look healthy for a while during the dormant period of winter. The first symptoms tend to show in spring - a blackening (or 'blasting') of blossoms, bud death, and the development of dark, sunken, rough and oval shaped cankers in the bark which exudes a watery gum substance. Nearby bark may develop reddish flecks, and the stressed rootstock may throw up suckers.

Organic control methods

This disease has no chemical cure. Prevention is the best measure - keep the tree healthy and unstressed by planting it in the right environment, protecting it from extreme weather conditions as much as possible and watering it if necessary.

BACTERIAL SPOT

Signs of Infection

Bacterial spot was first confirmed on almond trees in Australia in 1994/95. This disease affects stonefruit as well as almonds. Leaves develop red-brown 'shothole' shaped lesions, at sites of prolonged wetness. This includes the tips of leaves, the middle vein or the underside. Nuts will develop sunken, corky lesions that weep gum. Infected nuts and leaves are more likely to fall, causing crop loss, dieback and defoliation which can weaken the tree.

Organic Control Methods

Certain cultivars are more susceptible to bacterial spot than others - varieties to avoid include Fritz and Ne Plus.
Try to prevent the buildup excess of moisture by thinning the inner branches.

BANANA-SPOTTING BUG ON MACADAMIAS

Banana-spotting bug on macadamias - see Bananas.

BLACK PEACH APHID ON ALMONDS

Black Peach Aphid (*Brachycaudus persicae*) can affect almond trees. See the chapter on 'Stonefruit'.

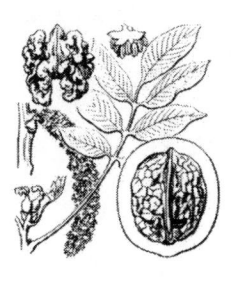

BLOSSOM BLIGHT

Blossom blight (*Botrytis cinerea*) is a common fungus that affects many fruit trees, vegetables and flowers, including almonds. It flourishes in times of high humidity and prolonged wet weather.

Signs of Infection

Infected blossoms die and become covered with gray fuzzy spores. Occasionally the fungus spreads to include unripe fruit and shoots.

Organic Control Methods

Use a fungicide (such as one of the ones listed towards the back of this book) to prevent and treat blossom blight. Be warned however that the fungus has some widespread resistant strains.

Pecan nut

MACADAMIA BLOSSOM BLIGHT

Blossom blight on macadamias is also known as Raceme blight or Grey blight.

Macadamia flower blights are caused by *Botrytis spp.* and *Phytophthora spp.*, in particular *Botrytis cinerea*.

It attacks plants when wet weather is combined with mild temperatures. It especially affects decaying petals in macadamia flowers, but it can also infect healthy buds and stalks.

Signs of Infection

Flower tissue turns brown and a gray mold grows over it.

Organic Control Methods

Usually it is best not to treat this disease, as it is possible for a large proportion of the macadamia racemes to become damaged without affecting the crop. This is because only a small percentage of these flowers ever become fruit.

Prevent the disease as much as possible by encouraging airflow through the orchard and the branches of the tree, through pruning. If necessary, a fungal spray should clear up the problem. See the chapter on 'Pest and Disease Remedies'

Macadamia nut

BROWN ROT

Brown rot is a sporadically appearing fungus that affects many plants, including stonefruit and almonds. The disease attacks the blossoms, during cool, misty or wet weather. Early flowering almonds are most susceptible as the early spring is usually when the ideal conditions for brown rot take place.

Signs of Infection

The affected blossoms wilt and wither, but remain clinging to the spur. The flowers may become covered in light brown spores, if conditions are humid enough. The rot usually spreads to the twig causing dieback.

Organic Control Methods

The fungus spores, once released, hide in buds, withered flowers, mummified fruit and twig cankers until wet conditions arise once more. Prevent the spread and return of this disease by spraying with a fungicide and removing all damaged and withering flowers and fruit.
Watering the tree during its blossom period can increase the likelihood of infection, so avoid this if you can.

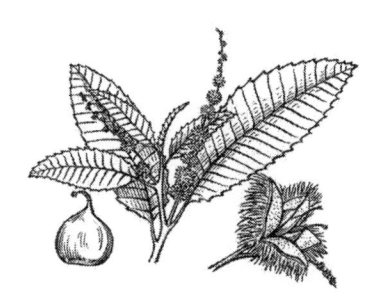

Chestnuts

BRYOBIA MITE

The Bryobia mite (*Bryobia rubrioculus*) feeds by piercing leaves' epidermal cells and sucking the contents. They are particularly prevalent in hot, dry conditions.

Signs of Infestation

The damaged leaves develop gray-white spots on the surface, where the mite has sucked the chlorophyll out of the cell. This impairs the leaf's ability to photosynthesise, weakening it. If the infestation is large, the vigour of the tree and hence the crop size may be reduced.

Organic Control Methods

Water-stressed trees are more susceptible to bryobia mite, so make sure to keep your almond tree well hydrated over summer. A winter oil spray during the dormant period is often an effective preventative. Applying dicofol to the tree is the best control when the infestation occurs in the growing season.

CAROB MOTH

The carob moth (*Apomyelois ceratoniae*) lays its eggs in the hulls of almonds, attracted by the scent of the fungi that often grows in the hulls when they start splitting. When the larvae hatch, they feed on the almond shells and kernels.

Signs of Infestation

Damage caused by the carob moth includes chewed almond kernels and grub-infested nuts.

Organic Control Methods

Spray regularly with an organic pesticide. Start when the hulls begin to split. See the chapters on Homemade and Commercial Remedies.

CROWN GALL

Crown gall is a bacterial disease that affects the roots of many woody plants, including almonds. Crown gall is most damaging to young trees. If a young tree develops galls, the tree will suffer, being less able to obtain water and nutrients. More established trees are less likely to be badly damaged. Young trees become stunted while older trees frequently develop other wood rots, because their resistance is lowered.

Signs of Infection

The bacteria survive in gall tissue and in soil. They enter only through wounds. Symptoms show up as rough, knobbly lumps on roots or trunk. Galls are soft and spongy. The centers of older galls rot away.

Organic Control Methods

Prevention is critical for this disease. 'Nemaguard' rootstocks are more susceptible to crown gall than peach-almond hybrid rootstocks.

When planting, use clean, uninfected soil and tools and try not to nick any roots or injure the tree in any way, because the bacteria enter through wounds. If you accidentally wound the tree, *resist* the temptation to paint the wound with 'tree wound sealant' or 'graft sealant'. Instead, paint wounds with a copper based paint or Bordeaux paste.

Wound sealants fail to stop rot or prevent decay organisms from entering the wound.

'Wound sealant/dressings' can harm trees because they –

- seal in moisture and decay
- frequently serve as a food source for pathogens
- prevent healthy new wood from forming
- inhibit the tree's natural resistance mechanisms for fighting insect attack or disease
- eventually crack, exposing the tree to fungi and bacteria

When pruning trees, dip all pruning tools in an effective disinfectant (eg methylated spirits) after each cut.

EUROPEAN RED MITE

See European Red Mite' (Panonychus ulmi) in General Fruit Pests and Diseases.

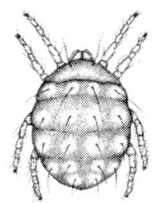

European red mite

FRUIT-SPOTTING BUG

Fruit-spotting bug (*Amblypelta nitida*) on macadamias - see General Fruit Pests and Diseases.

GREEN VEGETABLE BUG

Green vegetable bug (*Nezara viridula*) can affect macadamias. This is a flat, shield-shaped insect, 15mm long - with black or green nymphs spotted with orange, red and black.

Signs of Infestation

The green vegetable bug feeds on macadamia nuts, causing damage damage that is invisible until the nut is shelled - damage in the form of in the form of cottony-colored, circular spots or pitting on the surface of the kernel.

Organic Control Methods

Treat similarly to the fruit-spotting bug (see General Fruit Pests and Diseases).

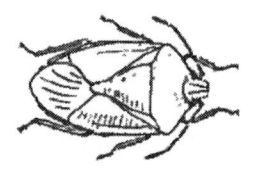

Green vegetable bug

HULL ROT

Hull rot (Rhizopus spp.) is a fungal disease that is most common in almonds in wet, warm conditions. When almond hulls are moist and open, it is easy for the fungus to enter and infect the nut.

Signs of Infection

Infected hulls display fungal growths, and nearby leaves and shoots wilt and die as the disease progresses.

Organic Control Methods

- Increase air movement in the canopy by pruning excess branches and twigs. Vigorous trees with interlacing branches and lots of leaves trap moisture and are most at risk for this disease.
- Avoid overhead irrigation during hull split.
- Although there are no resistant varieties of almond, some (such as Nonpareil) are more at risk than others.
- Unfortunately there is no effective chemical control for hull rot.

HUSK SPOT

Husk spot (*Psuedocercospora macadamiae*) is a fungal disease. It is one of the most serious threats to macadamia crops.

Spores enter the husk through the stomata, and spread during wet rainy weather.

Signs of Infection

Large irregular purple or brown spots develop on the unripe macadamia husks. Around the spots, the husk flesh turns yellow.

Infected nuts drop prematurely, giving poor kernel quality.

Organic Control Methods

Control has been achieved by applying organically-approved-fungicides such as copper sprays from early fruit set onwards. See Commercial and Home Made Remedies.

INDIAN MEAL MOTH

The Indian Meal Moth (*Plodia interpunctella*) feeds on almond kernels once they have been harvested and stored. They are also typically found in kitchens, feeding on flour.

Signs of Infestation

Infested nuts will become covered in dirty webbing that typically hangs in clumps. The moth is a mottled brown, and the larvae are dirty-white or yellow with brown heads.

Organic Control Methods

Dispose of infested material and remove all larvae and moths you can see. If the infestation is rather small, you can squish them by hand.
A home-made, all-purpose pesticide like a chilli spray can be used to kill and deter the moths. Moth traps can also be effective. Read more in the chapter on Home-made Pest Remedies.

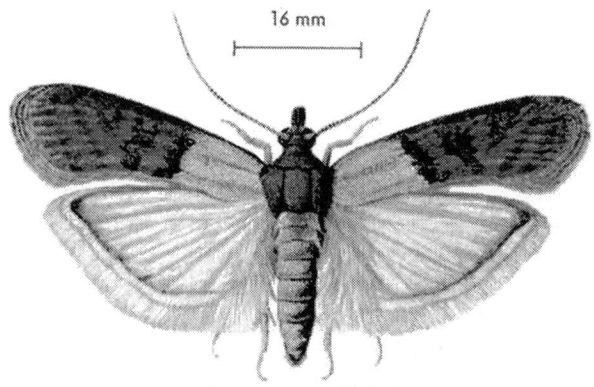

Indian Meal Moth

LEAF BLIGHT

Signs of Infection

This fungal disease (*Seimatosporium spp.*) is spread when rain splashes spores onto leaves. Almond trees can be affected. Infected leaves wither and drop off the tree, leaving the petioles behind.

Organic control methods

Treat as for 'shot hole'.

LIGHT BROWN APPLE MOTH

Light Brown Apple Moth (*Epiphyas postvittana*): see General Fruit Pests and Diseases.

MACADAMIA NUTBORER

Cryptophlebia ombrodelta, the macadamia nutborer, is a serious pest in Australia. It is a small, reddish-brown moth. It lays its eggs in Macadamian nuts, which subsequently hatch and feed on the tissue of the nut from within.

Fully-grown larvae construct tight, silken cocoons sealed with a flap, from which the moth emerges.

The macadamia nutborer is also a major insect pest of longan and lychee fruit, affecting these trees throughout their growing seasons.

Signs of Infestation

Upon hatching, the larvae bore holes through the nut's shell in search of food. When feeding on green fruit, the larva cause premature fruit drop; they may survive and mature in fallen fruit as well. When they feed on ripening fruit, it usually does not fall; the larvae often drown in the plant's juices.

The tissue surrounding the entrance hole may appear scalded (which is also the case with fruit fly infestations and leads to incorrect etiology). The damaged mature fruit often 'weeps,' staining other fruit in its cluster.

Organic Control Methods

Examine your macadamia fruit for signs of nutborer infestation. Spray with oganic pesticide if you find live, unhatched eggs. Check maturing fruit every week for larval entrance holes, keeping in mind that infestation levels tend to increase as the fruit matures.

The parasite *Trichgrammatoidea cryptophlebiae* has become well-established in Australia; this egg parasitoid provides effective biological control of the Macadamia nutborer. Several larval parasites also attack the borer, including the ichneumonid wasp, the braconid wasp, and a fly parasite (a tachinid) that has yet to be identified.

MACADAMIA FLOWER CATERPILLAR

Cryptoblabes hemigypsa is a gray moth, around 7mm long, with a wingspan of 14-18mm. Their tiny white-yellow eggs are laid on the racemes and are 0.5mm long. Larvae begin as yellow worm-like creatures, less than a millimetre long, but quickly grow and change color from yellow to green to a nearly-mature dark gray caterpillar around 12mm long.

Signs of Infestation

The flower caterpillar larvae feed on the macadamia racemes while the flowers are still in bud. The raceme becomes covered in webbing, faecal matter and the broken, decaying remains of chewed buds. An infestation can completely destroy a tree's racemes (and hence the crop).

Organic Control Methods

Spray with an organic insecticide (one with a low impact on beneficial insects), such as the ones in the chapters on 'Home Made and Commercial Pest Remedies'.

Monitor flower racemes regularly to check for the beginnings of infestation so it can be controlled with minimal damage.

MACADAMIA LEAFMINER

The macadamia leaf miner is the larva of a moth called *Acrocercops chionosema*. The small adult moth is less than half a centimetre long, with dark, white-barred forewings and plumed narrow hindwings.

Larvae are pale green and yellow, developing red bands when they are ready to pupate. They can grow up to 6mm long.

Signs of Infestation

The leaf mining looks like a large blotch on the leaf's upper side. Meandering trails weave beneath the surface of the leaf, and the leaf may show signs of blistering. When these blisters are moist it signifies the presence of a live larva sheltering underneath.

Organic Control Methods

Mature trees do not require any chemical treatment, as the damage is not going to negatively affect them. Only young trees that exhibit symptoms of leaf miner on 60% of leaves should be sprayed, and then with a registered organic insecticide.
Check trees regularly, and pluck off individually infested leaves. Encourage a garden population of biological controls, such as those described in Beneficial Predators.

MACADAMIA FELTED COCCID

Signs of Infestation

The Macadamia felted coccid (*Eriococcus ironsidei*) feeds on shoots and leaves. Young leaves will distort and stunt, while older leaves develop yellow spots, turn brown and fall off the tree. The undersides of the leaves hide liberal smatterings of small scales - gray females, brown male crawlers and white pupae. These insects may be present on the trunks and branches as well.

Organic Control Methods

Spray infested trees with an organic insecticide. Make sure you spray only the affected trees and trees growing nearby. Note that frequent use of some pesticides, even organic ones, destroys the natural predators of the felted coccid and may actually encourage build-up of the pest. Felted coccid usually finds it way into gardens and orchards via budwood or nursery plants. Make sure you carefully inspect all such materials. If you see signs of the pest, disinfest the plant material before use. Regularly check your trees so that you can treat the problem early, before it gets out of hand. Use mild organic pesticides with minimal impact on beneficial insects.

MACADAMIA TWIG-GIRDLER

Macadamia twig-girdlers are the larvae of the scale insect *Neodrepta luteotactella*. The larvae are mottled brown, similar in appearance to the macadamia nutborer, with rows of dark brown dots down the back and a black head.

Signs of Infestation

The first signs of damage caused by macadamia twig-girdler include the skeletonisation of leaves, which are webbed together together to form larval nests.

Organic Control Methods

Organic sprays are important to control the spread of this disease. See 'Scale and Sooty Mold' under General Fruit Pests.

SCALE INSECTS

Cause: Macadamia white scale (*Pseudaulacaspis brimblecombei*), long soft scale (*Coccus longulus*), macadamia mussel scale (*Lepidosaphes macadamiae*), oleander scale (*Aspidiotus nerii*) and latania scale (*Hemiberlesia lataniae*).

See 'Scale and Sooty Mold' in 'General Fruit Pests and Diseases'.

MIRID BUG

Mirid bug on cashew plants - 'see General Fruit Pests and Diseases'.

NEMATODES

See the chapter on 'General Fruit Pests and Diseases'.

PEACH SILVER MITE

Peach Silver mites (*Aculus cornutus*) can afflict peach, nectarine and almond trees.

Note: infestation by these mites should not be confused with a a fungal disease called Silver Leaf, which is caused by the pathogen *Chondrosterium purpureum*.

Signs of Infestation

The mites suck nutrients out of plant tissues, causing silvering of the foliage late in the season as well as yellow chlorotic spots on young leaves.

With heavy infestations the leaves curl and may fall, plant growth is stunted and crop yield declines.

Organic Control Methods

Peach silver mite is not affected by pyrethrum, ao avoid using this pesticide. Using pyrethrum may actually increase mite numbers by killing their natural enemies.

Peach silver mite appears to have several efficient natural enemies of the family *Phytoseiidae*. The mites serve as early season food for predatory mites, which in turn aid in reducing populations of other pest mites, so the best approach is to let nature take its course.

Sulfur sprays are acceptable for organically grown fruit and nuts, but will reduce predator mite populations.

PHYTOPHTHORA

Phytophthora, which means 'Plant Destroyer' in Latin, is a fungal disease that causes root and crown rot in almonds and walnuts.

Signs of Infection

The effect of *Phytophthora spp.* on root systems often remains unnoticed until the above-ground parts of the tree display symptoms. Symptoms of Phytophthora damage are poor tree vigor, loss of branches, and gumming or bleeding around the tree trunk.

Organic control methods

See the chapter on 'General Fruit Pests and Diseases'.

RUST

Rust (*Tranzschelia discolor*) can affect nut trees. See the chapter on 'General Fruit Pests and Diseases'.

RUST MITE

Rust mites (*Aculus spp.*) are minuscule insects that live under loose bark and bud scales during the winter dormant period, but move onto new leaves in spring to feed.

Signs of Infestation

Their feeding kills the leaves' epidermal cells, causing the leaf to turn a bronze color, dry out and distort.

Organic Control Methods

Organic oil sprays (such as 'White Oil') can be used to control this mite. See 'Homemade Remedies'.

SAN JOSE SCALE

San Jose Scale (*Diaspidiotus perniciosus*) can affect almond trees. See the chapter on 'General Fruit Pests and Diseases'.

SHOTHOLE

Shothole (*Wilsonomyces carpophilus*) is a fungal disease that affects an almond's leaves, flowers and fruit. Spores persist in twigs and buds, keeping them safe until in spring the rain can activate and splash the spores onto leaves and blossoms.

Signs of Infection

Purplish, circular spots develop on the leaves. These spots enlarge, and display a defined center surrounded by a margin of yellow. Eventually the center falls out, forming the 'shot holes' on the leaves. On fruit, lesions develop and become corky over time.

Organic Control Methods

Use a preventative fungal spray (such as one of the ones described towards the end of this book) and spray every few weeks after the tree's leaves first emerge to five or six weeks after the last blossom loses its petals.

SILVERLEAF

Silverleaf (*Chondrostereum purpureum*) is a fungal disease that can affect nut trees. See 'Silverleaf' under Stonefruit.

TRUNK CANKER

Trunk canker (*Phytophthora cinnamomi*) is a disease that can affect macadamias. It is caused by one of the many forms of phytophthora that parasitize a variety of host trees and other plants. In macadamia nut trees, their effects are rather more specialised.

Signs of Infection

Leaves turn yellow and brown, causing massive defoliation. Lesions may appear on the roots and trunk, spreading to the branches if the disease is advanced. The rootstock may start suckering. Mature trees will often become dehydrated, and will drop their crop.

Organic Control Methods

See 'Phytophthora' in the chapter on 'General Fruit Pests and Diseases'.

TWO-SPOTTED SPIDER MITE

Two-Spotted Spider Mite (*Tetranychus urticae*): see General Fruit Pests and Diseases.

VERTICILLIUM WILT

Verticillium Wilt (*Verticillium dahliae*) is a fungal plant pathogen. See 'Verticillium Wilt' in the chapter on 'Stonefruit'.

WALNUT BLIGHT

Walnut blight (*Pseudomonas juglandis*) is a disease striking new growth and nuts in wet weather.

Signs of Infection

Also known as 'bacterial blight,' walnut blight causes small black spots to appear on young leaves, which in turn leads to larger areas of infection. It results in withering, dieback of shoots, and damage to fruit.

The *P. juglandis* bacterium overwinters in dormant buds that appear to be healthy; this leads to reinfection of young growth.

Organic Control Methods

- Cut out all infected parts well back from visibly damaged areas and burn them.
- Use Bordeaux mixture to prevent reinfection.
- It may help to keep the soil pH higher than 6.
- Guard against overfeeding the plant with nitrogen
- Sufficiently prune your walnut tree to provide plenty of openings for aeration.

12

PAWPAWS

'Pawpaw' can refer to the plants and fruit of at least three different genera.

- *Carica papaya*, the widely cultivated pawpaw (also called papaya or papaw), is a tropical fruit tree.
- Mountain pawpaw/papaya (*Vasconcellea pubescens*) is native to South America. It can grow in temperate climates.
- The Eastern North American pawpaw's botanical name is *Asimina triloba*. Like the mountain pawpaw, it can grow in temperate climates.

Pawpaw trees grow quickly, producing large crops of delicious fruit that can be used in a myriad sweet or savory dishes. They are ideal for smaller gardens due to their compact size.

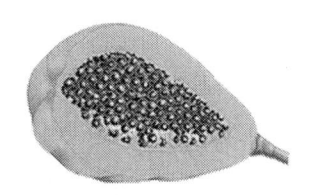

PAWPAW MOSAIC VIRUS

Pawpaw mosaic virus targets pawpaw trees, entering the sap through the wounds created by sap sucking insects or infected garden equipment (such as secateurs).

Signs of Infection

It can be identified through the characteristic pale mosaic' mottling effect on the leaves.

Organic Control Methods

Infected plants must be destroyed. Since viruses will not infect the soil the diseased plant can be composted.
Garden tools should be disinfected using bleach, methylated spirits or tree tree oil.

FUNGAL DISEASES

Two fungal diseases may affect pawpaws. They most commonly occur in regions with high rainfall and high humidity.

Black spot (*Asperisporum caricae*). This disease makes the fruit look unsightly. It also decreases the overall vigour of the tree by reducing the ability of the leaves to photosynthesize. Plants are more susceptible in cooler months.

Signs of Infection

Black spots develop on the underside of the leaves. Eventually the leaves turn brown and fall off. Large black 'necrotic' spots also appear on fruits, which begin to rot.

Anthracnose (*Colletotrichium gloeaporides*). This disease spreads via water droplets or infected seed. It is more severe in warm, humid weather.

Signs of Infection

Dark, sunken, watery patches appear on the pawpaws. Pinkish spore masses may form on the spots. They expand, rapidly rotting and spoiling large areas of the fruit.
The fungal lesions can also affect harvested fruit if the anthracnose has taken hold.

Organic Control Methods of Fungal Diseases

Both fungal diseases can be treated the same way.

- Check before you buy pawpaw plants that they are healthy and free of diseases.

- Plant pawpaws in the best position. Pawpaws prefer a well-mulched soil that is free-draining. Avoid planting them close to other plants because free air flow will help to prevent fungal spores from spreading.

- Prepare your soil. Pawpaws are susceptible to nutrient deficiencies. These weaken the plant and renders them more vulnerable to fungal attacks. Black spot often attacks pawpaws that are deficient in potassium, phosphorus and magnesium. Anthracnose affected plants are frequently lacking in calcium and nitrogen.

- Check the pH of your soil. The wrong pH can 'lock-up' nutrients. Pawpaws do not thrive in acid soils. If your garden experiences long periods of rain (which acidifies soil), you may need to 'sweeten' the soil with dolomite.

- Place a thick layer of mulch around your pawpaw trees. This will help to stop the nutrients from leaching away. It will also add nutritious organic matter. Lucerne mulch is excellent for increasing potassium and potash levels.

- Sprinkle some Epsom salts on the ground arounf your pawpaw. Epsom salts is magnesium sulphate, which will help remedy any magnesium deficiency.

- Regularly feed your pawpaws. Pawpaws need regular feeding with a good organic fertilizer. Apply aged chicken manure and rock dust. Give your pawpaws a drink of trace elements after heavy rain. Regular liquid feeding with seaweed fertilizer is recommended to stimulate root growth.

- If your plants are infected, dig them out and plant healthy pawpaws in a sunny, well-ventilated part of the garden. Destroy all infected plants.

- Prune your pawpaws. You can cut pawpaws back quite hard, almost to ground level, and they will re-shoot from the main stem.

- When your plants show a flush of new growth, apply a preventative spray of a copper based fungicide.

POSSUMS, RATS AND GRASSHOPPERS

Signs of Infestation

The leaves are damaged and shrivelled. When the fruit grows, it will appear chewed and gnawed.

Organic Control Methods

See our sections on rats, possums and grasshoppers in 'General Fruit Pests and Diseases'.

13

PEARS

CODLING MOTH

Codling moth is a common pest of pears. See the chapter on 'General Fruit Pests and Diseases'.

EUROPEAN RED MITE

See the chapter on 'General Fruit Pests and Diseases' under 'European Red Mite'

MEALYBUGS

See 'Mealybugs' under 'General Fruit Pests and Diseases'.

ORIENTAL FRUIT MOTH

Oriental fruit moth (*Cydia molesta*) is closely related to the codling moth. It attacks young pear shoots and fruit, but also affects stonefruit, quinces and apples.

The small, gray adults are rarely seen in daylight, but can sometime be observed in mating flights in the late afternoon on warm spring days. Small, round, cream-colored eggs are then laid on the twigs and leaves of the tree.

The caterpillar larvae will burrow into shoot tips and feed. Four weeks later, the mature larva is around 12 mm long and pink with brown head. It will start to seek out a safe place to cocoon - such as a bit of loose bark or leaf litter somewhere in the fork of a branch near where it has been feeding.

After cocooning, the larva pupates immediately, and emerges as an adult moth in late spring or summer. Later generations, instead of attacking shoots, will feed on fruit and new leaves.

Over the warm months, the orchard may see 5-6 overlapping generations of Oriental moth as the moth lifecycle is around 33 days. The last generation of the season will cocoon and lie dormant under bark in the base of the tree or in leaf litter on the ground until the cold months have passed.

Signs of Infestation

Affected shoots will produce gum, wilt and die, stunting tree growth. Fruit damage is similar to that of the codling moth – brown trails and rotten patches in the fruit where the larvae have fed. This can destroy a crop.

Organic Control Methods

Infested twigs should be cut off (to the length of 20 cm) and burned as soon as wilting becomes apparent.

Similar to the codling moth, it is expedient to remove loose bark and debris from branches and leaf litter beneath the tree to reduce places for the larvae to hide. At the same time, apply a corrugated cardboard band to the trunk (with a grease band beneath) to trap larvae and pupae - this cardboard band should be checked regularly and the cocoons and larvae destroyed.

Check all fruit regularly for the tiny holes that signify infestation, as for the codling moth. Infested fruit must be destroyed - put them in a sealed black plastic bag and leave in the sun for a few days before feeding them to animals or composting.

If you have chickens and mature trees let them roam around and forage in the orchard - they will feed on any larvae and damaged fruit. This should not be done with young trees however as their delicate root systems may be damaged by hen scratching.

The natural predators of the Oriental fruit moth include the ichneumon wasp *Glarbridorsum stokesii* and the *Trichogramma* micro-wasp - both of which parasitize the moth eggs. The Trichogramma can be purchased and released in the garden to control moth populations. Encourage these populations to flourish by planting flowers high in pollen and nectar beneath the trees - such as clover, mustard, Queen Anne's lace, alyssum, dill and coriander.

Other predators include chalcid wasps, braconid wasps, tachinid flies, caradbid beetles, ants, spiders and earwigs - as well as night flying birds, tree frogs and insectivorous bats. To help them get into the tree and feed on the moth larvae, prune dense growth from the tree each year.

Thin large fruit crops to avoid fruit touching each-other, as this helps the larvae spread.

PEAR SCAB

Pear scab is a fungal disease caused by *Venturia pirina,* which causes similar blemishes on pear fruit and leaves as apple scab does to apples.

The pear scab pathogen spends the winter dormant in the leaf-litter (or sometimes in lesions on infected twigs). In spring, the ascospores are released, either by rainwater or sprinkler irrigation.

These 'primary spores' are splashed up or carried by the wind to infect healthy leaves, flowers or fruit. Between 8 and 17 days after primary infection, the fungus produces condida (secondary spores), which help the disease spread. Wet conditions are necessary for the fungus to spread.

Signs of Infection

The first sign of pear scab takes the form of yellow spots on the leaves. Later, darker olive-colored spots develop on the leaves, fruit and (if the infection is severe) stems. On the underside of the leaves the spots may appear velvety (this is caused by the fungal growths).

The affected leaves will often pucker and distort. In severe cases this may affect all the leaves on the tree. Eventually the leaves may turn yellow and fall off, causing defoliation. Blossom drop may also occur if the scab infects the flower stems.

On the fruit, the 'scabs' for which the disease is known will form. These take the form of velvety gray-black lesions (often with a red halo) that later become sunken tan indents. The fruit may crack (allowing other pests to enter) or distort, causing it to fall from the tree.

Scab can cause severe damage and destruction to the pear crop - either through blossom drop or malformation and cracking of the fruit. Defoliation can occur, weakening the tree. Generally early infection is more destructive than late infection, as late-infected fruit can often be salvaged by simply peeling the skin.

Organic Control Methods

Regularly rake and remove fallen leaves, composting or destroying them away from the trees.

To hasten leaf-fall in autumn, apply urea to the leaves, then add lime to the leaf piles under the tree to kill the dormant fungus.

Avoid creating prolonged wet conditions that encourage the growth of the fungus. For example, if using a sprinkler, adjust the angle to avoid wetting the leaves, and irrigate during the morning so as to allow enough time for drying.

In rainy weather (where the leaves are likely to stay wet for nine hours or more), it may be necessary to apply a fungicide spray. This should be done as soon as the tips of the leaves appear, and repeated as soon as the (unopened) blossom clusters emerge (around two weeks later).

A third treatment may be required after the petals fall, to prevent the young fruit from being affected. As leaves and fruit mature, they become less susceptible to scab infection, but occasionally they may be targeted by secondary infection. Preventing the prrimary infection however will usually take care of that.

Appropriate organic fungicides include copper and Bordeaux (which should only be used during the period between the first emergence of leaf-tips and full bloom as spraying on fruit can cause fruit russetting), as well as sulfur, mineral and neem oils.

Some pear cultivars are relatively resistant to scab - these include Asian pear varieties and European cultivars such as Arganche, Batjarka, Brandy, Muscat, and Passe Crassane, among others.

PEAR LEAF BLISTER MITE

The blisters that sometimes appear on pear leaves are actually caused by tiny, microscopic gall mites.

Signs of Infection

Pear leaf blister mite (*Eriophyes pyri or Phytoptus pyri*) is characterised by a pattern of blotches on the plant leaves - light pink or yellow-green and slightly indented on the upper surface, while the underside is spotted with black, raised marks. These 'blisters' warp the shape of the leaves.

Organic control methods

No effective organic remedy has been found for this problem, except possibly plucking off the affected leaves. Fortunately, pearleaf blister mites do little but make the plant more unsightly.

SAN JOSE SCALE

See the chapter on 'General Fruit Pests and Diseases'.

THRIPS

See 'Thrips' under 'General Fruit Pests and Diseases'.

TWO-SPOTTED MITE

See 'Two-spotted mite' in the chapter on 'General Fruit Pests and Diseases'.

14

STONEFRUIT

Stonefruits such as peaches, nectarines, plums, apricots, and cherries are all related, belonging to the genus Prunus.

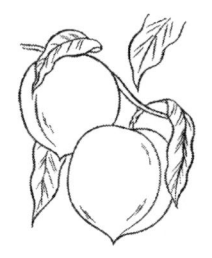

BLACK PEACH APHID

The black peach aphid (*Brachycaudus persicae*) has a winged and a wingless form. The wingless form spends the winter feeding on roots, then migrate in spring up the tree to the leaves, shoots and buds in spring.

Winged adults are born in summer, and fly to other trees. By midsummer, the wingless forms have migrated back underground to feed again on the roots. Both winged and wingless adults are tiny (2mm), and are shiny black in color, while immature nymphs are red-brown.

Signs of Infestation

The main damage cause by the black peach aphid is root damage by the wingless adults during the tree's dormant period. If root feeding occurs on young trees, this can severely stunt growth and reduce the tree's resistance to other pests, diseases and environmental damage.

During spring and summer, the above-ground damage is seldom serious. Affected leaves may curl, turn yellow and fall off, and sometimes fruit distortion occurs, but not usually on a widespread scale. As with all aphids, honeydew excretion can lead to the growth of sooty mold.

Organic Control Methods

Biological control methods are the most important here – encourage beneficial insects like ladybeetles and lacewings to take residence in the garden. See the chapter on 'Beneficial Predators' for more information.
Spraying with white oil can also kill aphids.

CHERRY FRUITWORM

Grapholita packardi overwinters in its larval state in small cavities in dead wood. The dark-gray moths emerge in the spring, recognizable by their brown, banded wings. The eggs are then laid on the undersurfaces of leaves and on the fruit.

After hatching, the larvae enter the cherries and feed on them one by one. They seal with silk the holes through which they enter the fruit.

Signs of Infestation

A cherry fruitworm infestation is indicated by shrunken berries that are prematurely ripe. The fruit will then rot on the vine, greatly reducing fruit yields. While cherry fruitworms enter the fruit through wounds from the outside, the greater damage is done from within.

Organic control methods

- To control cherry fruitworms, kill them when the eggs are being laid in the late spring. Choose an organic pesticide that is safe for bees, as they are abundant at that time and are needed for pollination.

- The insecticide of choice for cherry fruitworms is Bacillus thuringiensis (BT), a bacterium used as a biological pesticide. In moderate sprayings, it is harmless to bees.

- Fruitworms can also be controlled with broad spectrum insecticides. They should be applied at petal fall to avoid toxicity to bees. Remove any bee hives prior to insecticide spraying.

- A second spray is recommended in about ten days.

COLLAR ROT

Collar rot is a other fungal disease that attacks stonefruit trees such as peaches, apricots and cherries. Technically speaking, genuine collar rot strikes only the trunk scion near grafts. The term is often used, however, to indicate the much more prevalent infection of roots or rootstock crowns.
Collar rot is described in more detail in the 'Citrus' chapter.

CURLY LEAF

Fungal diseases can cause spotting and shriveling on both leaves and fruit. If left untreated, they can cause widespread defoliation and crop loss.
These diseases can be controlled using a copper-based fungicide such as cupric hydroxide. Spray during still, windless days and when spraying, do not neglect the leaf undersides.

Curly leaf (sometimes known as peach leaf curl) is a fungal disease caused by the organism *Taphrina deformans*.

It damages and distorts leaves, shoots, blossoms and fruit belonging to peaches or nectarines. It one of the most common peach diseases, usually occurring in wet, cool conditions.

Curly leaf can significantly reduce the tree's fruit yield, and if left untreated for several years, may cause extreme defoliation and kill the tree.

Signs of Infection

One of the first signs of curly leaf is the development of red patches on the new spring leaves. These red areas thicken, causing the leaf to pucker, curl and distort. The thick patches then turn yellow develop gray fungal spores on the surface.

Eventually the leaves will turn completely yellow or brown, and may fall to the ground. To replace them, the tree may produce a second set of leaves - the growth of which uses up valuable nutrients that would otherwise go into fruit. As a result, the fruit production is decreased.

If defoliation is widespread, it may lead to sunburn on the branches of the tree. The fungus may also cause shoots to thicken, distort and become stunted or die.

Occasionally fruit may also become infected, developing reddish, wrinkled or lumpy patches on the fruit's surface, which will eventually crack and become corky.

Organic Control Methods

- Some peach and nectarine varieties are resistant to curly leaf. These include Redhaven, Indian Free, Q-1-8 and Muir (for peaches) and Kreibich (for nectarines).
- Remove all damaged leaves from the tree, and rake up all fallen leaves. Burn or otherwise dispose of these leaves far from any stonefruit trees.
- During autumn (after the leaves have fallen), drench the tree with a copper-based spray in sufficient quantities that the liquid drips off the tree. This is to ensure the spray reaches all cracks and crevices where fungal spores hide.
- Repeat this process in the middle of winter and in early spring just before bud burst.

SCALE INSECTS

See 'Scale and Sooty Mold' in 'General Fruit Pests and Diseases'.

SILVERLEAF

Silverleaf (*Chondrostereum purpureum*) is a destructive, wood-rotting fungus that attacks the xylem (water-drawing) tissue of many stonefruit, as well as almond trees and pome fruit.
It attacks most species of the family Rosaceae, particularly the genus Prunus. Plums are especially vulnerable.

The disease spreads when the fungal spores land on fresh tree wounds or cuts, since this is how they access the xylem. For this reason it is vital to prune cherries and plums in summer, when spores are least likely to be present and when disease is visible.

The disease is fatal. The tree usually dies within three seasons, as the fungus releases a toxin, poisoning the plant slowly.

Signs of Infection

The development of the ubiquitous silvery color on the leaves of the tree is the first sign of silverleaf. The effects can be confused with the paling of leaves caused by a mite infestation. However, cutting a cross section of a twig from a tree infected with silverleaf should show the xylem stained dark with the disease.

The fruiting bodies of this fungus are fan shaped and colored mauve-brown. They develop on dead and infected wood, (such as stumps and piles of pruned branches), or on other living hosts like willows.

Organic control methods

Unfortunately there is no cure for this disease. Remove the tree and burn or bury it. Check all surrounding trees for the presence of the purplish fruiting bodies. Try to prevent infection occurring in the first place by only pruning on dry, sunny days.

VERTICILLIUM WILT

Also known as blackheart, this fungal disease is a global phenomenon, although it is most often found in the world's relatively temperate zones. Apricots are perhaps its most common victim, followed by other stonefruit (nectarines and peaches, for example). Verticillium also attacks various nut trees, such as walnut, almond and chestnut.

Signs of Infection
Verticillium wilt *Verticillium dahliae*} causes ongoing leaf loss beginning at each limb's base, usually beginning in the early part of summer. Infected leaves usually yellow and lose their luster; soon thereafter, they will prematurely drop from the tree. Severely infected limbs often retain only a hint of leaves by the end of summer.

Verticillium is a fairly serious threat to commercial stonefruit harvesting; even if the infected trees take many years to die, they will tend to yield stunted, substandard fruit. Unfortunately, trees planted to replace infected trees have a high likelihood of eventually becoming infected themselves. For the backyard grower, it means an unsatisfying fruit yield.

This wilt may survive in soil for years, both as a root parasite of various weeds and plants and a resting body. The point of attack in healthy plants is usually a wounded section of the tree or through the 'hairs' of its root system.

It tends to proceed to grow within the wood, and to form spores. Through the water conducted in the wood, the spores move upward in the direction of the stems and their leaves. The disease ascends vertically, causing a continuous section of affected wood throughout the tree.

Organic control methods

Verticillium is known to be among the more control-resistant fungal infections plaguing stonefruit trees. This is largely a function of the infection's source: the soil, where nutrients are always on hand to feed the fungus.

Prevention is of paramount importance. Gardeners must find ways of starving the fungus in the soil before it has the chance to spread to the tree and begin its steady, upward destruction.

Plant new stonefruit trees in soil that has lain under grass and weeds for some time – ideally, for a number of years. The last thing you want to do is to plant a stonefruit tree in soil that has recently hosted strawberries or tomatoes; such earth provides fertile ground for nascent *Verticillium dahliae*.

Be sure to use only high-quality, uninfected planting stock, as Verticillium often spreads through low-quality vegetative stock.

Additionally, you may wish to plant pears or apples in V. dahliae-infected soil; both are known for their resistance to the fungus. Apricots may be more successfully cultivated using plum rootstock, as this shows a marked resistance to V. dahliae as well.

Backyard stonefruit growers also do well to avoid planting young trees near melons, peppers and potatoes, any of which may increase the presence of the fungus in the soil.

To prevent such an increase, keep weed growth under control and try to allow only clover and grass to remain. Weeds of various kinds – notably nightshade and amaranthus – are prevalent *V. dahliae* hosts.

It is important to do a thorough job of infected tree and root removal once Verticillium has asserted itself. Instead of fumigation, consider solarisation of the soil; this is an excellent, all-natural way of killing fungal remnants prior to replacing the tree.

Verticillium is one of those fungi that thrive on an overabundance of fertilizer, so fertilize judiciously. Condition your soil properly with adequate organic matter. Damage to the root structure and water stress can both contribute substantively to Verticillium wilt infection as well.

15

QUINCES

Common Quince (Cydonia oblonga)

Quinces have few major pests and diseases. Their main pests: fruit fly, codling moth and pear and cherry slug are all covered in the chapter on 'General Fruit Pests and Diseases'.

FLECK

Quince fleck fungus (*Fabrea maculata*) is a disease which affects quinces in particularly in warm, coastal regions. If left uncontrolled, fleck can defoliate the entire tree, and destroy the crop.

Signs of Infection

Quinces are usually infected in spring, as the new leaves develop. Fleck manifests as small, purplish bumpy spots on the leaves, with a white dot in the center of each. As the disease progresses, these spots turn dark brown, ash-gray or red-brown, enlarging and merging together, covering large areas of the leaves and causing them to fall.

Fleck forms dark brown spots on the fruit, which grow, becoming black and sunken, warping and sometimes cracking the fruit and causing it to fall prematuring. Lesions develop on the shoots, which are harder to see.

Organic Control Methods

Certain quince varieties are more resistant to fleck than others. Resistant varieties include De Vranja, Appleshapeed, Smyrna and De Bourgeaut.

Affected trees should be sprayed with an organic fungicide.

Fallen leaves should be regularly raked and disposed of away from the tree (e.g. burnt).

Open the tree up to air circulation and avoid the wet conditions that encourage fleck by pruning all dead wood.

FRUIT FLY AND CODLING MOTH

Fruit fly and codling moth can be controlled through recommended pest control strategies for apples and pears, see 'General Fruit Pests and Diseases'.

PEAR AND CHERRY SLUG

See the chapter on 'General Fruit Pests and Diseases'.

QUINCE LEAF BLIGHT

Quince leaf blight is caused by the fungus *Diplocarpon mespili*. Particularly wet summer weather induces the growth of the fungus. It causes unsightly spots on leaves, and saps the vigor from the tree.

Signs of Infection

Quince leaf blight manifestst as small, dark spots with gray at the center. These coalesce into larger splotches, turning the leaves yellow or brown; eventually, they will prematurely fall from the tree. You get some shoot tip dieback with a quince infection, and the fruit may become distorted and blemished.

Organic Control Methods

Rake up all affected leaves and dispose of them as soon as possible. Prune dead shoots while the tree is dormant, and maintain excellent cultivation, helping your tree to regrow foliage.

16

BENEFICIAL PREDATORS

ABOUT BENEFICIAL PREDATORS

Not all insects in the garden are there to attack your plants. Quite the contrary! Many are there to prey on the ones that eat your leaves and fruits. We call them beneficial predators, or 'good bugs'.

Beetles and bugs are large insect groups which include many pests. Importantly for the health of the garden, many of the natural predators of insect pests are bugs and beetles.

Bugs and beetles are not interchangeable, but very different kinds of mini-beasts. Beetles have mandibles (pincer-like mouthparts for gripping and chewing), while bugs have sucking mouthparts. Beetles have pupal stages while bugs do not.

Parasitic insects lay their eggs on or inside the bodies or eggs of their 'host' insect. When the eggs hatch, the larvae eat the host alive. Usually parasites will only target a particular species of insect.

Not only insects but also mammals, birds, reptiles and amphibians can be your garden helpers. By encouraging them to live in your garden you are getting them to help control the damaging bugs.

Green Lacewing

BENEFICIAL INSECTS

Green Lacewings (*Mallada signata*)
While the adult lacewings feed only on plant nectar, their larvae are great aphid predators, able to consume hundreds of pests each per week.

Hoverflies (*Syrphidae spp.*)
Hoverflies are also known as Flower Flies or Syrphid Flies. The larvae of this bee-resembling insect are great aphid-eaters, and will prey on many varieties of soft-bodied insect pest.

Ladybirds/Ladybugs/Ladybeetles (*Coccinellidae spp.*)
While any gardener can recognize the adults of this friendly insect, the larvae may be difficult to identify. Ladybug larvae have black, elongated bodies with ridges and several patches of red or orange.
Ladybugs can be purchased commercially to add to a garden. If this is done, do not release them during the day as they will fly away - wait until evening or just before dawn. Before releasing, place the ladybeetles in the fridge for a couple of hours, to slow them down so they don't rush off and can take the time to get used to their new garden environment.
Ensure that your garden has plenty of food sources, water and shelter. Release them near a plant with aphids, or a flowering plant which has had its leaves sprayed with water.

Praying Mantises (*Mantis religiosa*)
The praying mantis/mantid is an example of a good bug. Praying mantises hunt for grasshoppers. In warmer climates you can attract praying mantises by planting a cinnamon tree.
The praying mantis will only eat meat that it has hunted down itself. Dedicated carnivores, they are completely harmless to plants. They have a voracious appetite, especially the young

newly hatched nymphs. They'll eat aphids, but will also eat any other creature small enough, including beneficial insects and other praying mantises.

Predatory mites (*Phtyoseiulus persimilis*)
Predatory mites eat young thrips and pest mites. They can be distinguished from other mites by their red or yellow color, and their rapid movement.

Robber flies (*Family Asilidae*)

Adult robber flies can be mistaken for dragonflies because they have similar characteristics. However, robber flies have only one pair of wings. They hold these over their backs when resting, unlike dragonflies, who have two pairs and hold them out to the side.
Adult robber flies feed on other insects. Larvae of robber flies live in soil or decomposing wood. The larvae of some species of robber flies are also predacious.

BENEFICIAL ARACHNIDS

Spiders (*Order Araneae*)
The numbers of plant-eating insects they eat makes spiders important to pest population control. Most spiders do not damage garden plants. Some spiders use webs to catch their prey, others hunt and catch it.

Most spiders are shy, and harmless to human beings. Spraying plants with water from a hose is often sufficient to remove spiders from plants prior to harvest.

BENEFICIAL AMPHIBIANS

Frogs (*Order Anura*)
Frogs eat many insects - including flies, mosquitoes, cockroaches and centipedes. The presence of frogs in a garden is considered an 'indicator' of environmental health.
Attracting frogs requires a source of water such as a pond, and a good mixture of water plants.

BENEFICIAL REPTILES

Garden Skinks (*Lampropholis guichenoti*)
Garden skinks are small brown lizards (ranging in size from 5-30cm long), commonly seen in gardens in temperate, subtropical and tropical regions.
Skinks hunt many small to large invertebrates - from moths and flies to ants and beetles.
To make your garden a safe place for skinks, keep some spaces where grass or other plants are long and provide cover for them to hunt.
Logs, bricks and stones can also provide protection for skinks to hide from their main predators (birds and cats).

BENEFICIAL BIRDS

Many birds are attracted to insects and flowers. Plant a diverse range of nectar-bearing flowers to bring a variety of insects and birds into your garden.

Chickens and ducks love to hunt for slugs, flies, caterpillars and snails. At the same time they provide fertilizer with their droppings.

ATTRACTING BENEFICAL PREDATORS

Plants that encourage 'good bugs' include:

Carrot Family
- Coriander (Coriandrum sativum), also known as cilantro. Sow Coriander seed all over your vegetable garden beds and then plant over. Many beneficial insects will visit the flowers.
- Queen Anne's Lace (Daucus carota). This is a compactand pretty plant that is excellent for attracting predatory insects.
- Giant Flat-leaved Italian Parsley (Petroselinum crispumvar.) One of the best predator attracting plants, this flowers copiously over a long period. Its nectar attracts wasps which parasitize leaf-eating caterpillars.
- Bronze Fennel (Foeniculum vulgare 'Purpureum.') The flowers attract predators.
- Dill Will flower almost all year round in warmer climates and its flowers are an excellent lure for parasitic flies that can control caterpillars. Dill is also a delicious herb.

Daisy Family
- Golden Rod (Solidago sp.) Flowers consistently. A very ornamental plant that attracts beneficial insects to your garden and provides egg-laying habitats for them.
- Cosmos. Like all plants in the daisy family, cosmos provide plenty of pollen. This is like a magnet for hover flies, whose young prey on aphids.

Mint Family
- The mint family, with its delicious pollen and nectar, appeals to a huge range of beneficial predators. It's also a useful culinary plant.

Other ways to lure a variety of beneficial predators:

- Offer them a range of plants that can give them shelter and food. Provide ground cover in the form of low-growing plants (such as thyme or oregano) to protect beneficial insects from predators like birds.
- A layer of mulch will also provide cover for these insects and will benefit the plants by preventing the soil from drying out and protecting roots from heat stress.
- An artificial insect attractant made from water, sugar and brewer's yeast sprayed onto leaves will attract nectar-loving beneficial insects.
- Refrain from spraying poisons around; you don't want to kill the good guys.
- Allow a few pests to wander around so that the predators can get a meal. Ultimately you will be rewarded with less work spraying, and a better harvest.
- Fill shallow dishes with a layer of small rocks or pebbles. Add water to cover the bottom half of the rocks. Place the dishes on the ground around your garden. Beneficial creatures will visit to have a drink of water.
- Build a pond to attract frogs.

MAKE A LADYBEETLE FEEDER

To make your garden even more appealing to ladybeetles, make a feeder and keep it stocked with fresh tidbits.

Materials:
- Bamboo, about 25cm (10') in length by 4 - 5 cm (1 1/2' - 2' in) diameter.
- Garden twine or chain
- Fresh raisins that have been soaked in water for a few minutes, or small dabs of honey.

Tools
- Saw
- Drill
- Pencil
- Ruler
- Sandpaper

Instructions:

- Measure a section of bamboo to be about 25cm (10') long and make a mark there with the pencil.

- Use your pencil to draw a line tapering the end at an angle. This will provide a tiny 'verandah' to keep the rain out of your ladybeetle feeder.

- Use your saw to cut the line at the angle, being careful not to split your bamboo.

- Do the same thing on the opposite end. If the ends are really sharp or jagged, you can gently sand them with a piece of sandpaper.
-
- Drill holes just slightly bigger than the twine you're using.

- Insert twine ends through the holes, making a double knot on each end. Your twine should last through the season but might need to replaced yearly.

- Hang your ladybeetle feeder from a fence or a hook on a pole or the branch of a tree, and insert a couple of raisins into the bamboo feeder. The raisins will draw the ladybeetles to the feeder and feed them if aphids or other insects are scarce.

- You might decide to hang it close to a food source, such as near aphid infested rose bushes.

17

PEST AND DISEASE REMEDIES

HOME MADE ORGANIC REMEDIES

Note: Some plants may be sensitive to these mixtures - for all homemade recipes it is advisable to test a small amount of the solution on a few leaves of the plant 24 hours before widespread use, to make sure it won't casue damage.

Horticultural Oil/White Oil (Version 1)
This easy home-made oil is extremely useful on most insects, acting to suffocate or dry them out. Create a soap-oil concentrate by combining two cups of vegetable oil with half a cup of dishwashing detergent and shaking it up in a jar. Add two tablespoons of the mix to a litre of water for an easy spray.

- Can be used on: most insects, such as scale, aphids, whiteflies, leaf miners, mealybugs and mites.

Horticultural Oil/White Oil (Version 2)
Mix a cup of vegetable oil with a few millilitres of potassium soap and one and a half cups of water. Mix with ten parts water before spraying.

- Can be used on: see above.

Coffee Spray
Combine black espresso coffee with water at the ratio 1:10. Spray on soil and leaves to deter snails and slugs.

- Can be used on: slugs and snails.

All-round insecticide
Chop up four onions, two cloves of garlic and four chillies - mix with hot soapy water and let steep for 12 hours. Strain off the liquid and mix with five litres of water.

- Can be used on: all insects.

Soap Spray
Mix two tablespoons of soap flakes with a litre of water then spray the solution onto plants.

- Can be used on: aphids and caterpillars.

Pawpaw Spray
Blend pawpaw leaves and water until they form a thick paste. Mix with a litre of boiling water and let stand for several hours before straining and adding two more litres of water, 30ml of potassium soap and 6ml of vegetable oil. Stir and strain.

- Can be used on: soft-bodied insects such as mites and aphids.

Chilli Spray
Blend Birdseye chillies with water to make a paste (being careful not to breathe the irritating fumes or let the chillies get on the face or eyes). Add a litre of water and 10ml of potassium soap before letting it stand for 12 hours.

- Can be used on: all insects except beetles and grasshoppers.

Potassium Soap Spray

This is a gentler soap spray than others mentioned above. You can purchase soaps that contain potassium hydroxide from soap-making suppliers. Combine 20ml of soap with a litre of water.

Note:
- Do not use soaps that contain lye (sodium hydroxide).
- Do not use chlorinated water.
- Do not use detergents such as liquid dish soap. Unlike soap, which is organic, detergents are chemical cleaners and are toxic to most plants.

- Can be used on: small, soft-bodied insects like thrips, aphids, mites, white flies, mealybugs, and immature scales. This spray also destroys small larvae and eggs, including those of moths, flies, and beetles.

Barriers

Crushed roughage can prevent crawling pests from reaching your precious plants. An effective barrier can be made from wood ash, crushed eggshells or ground coffee.

- Can be used to deter: snails and slugs.

Beer Trap for Snails and Slugs

Fill a small jar half-full of beer and sit it in the ground so that the lip of the jar just protrudes above the soil. The yeast in the beer will attract snails and slugs, which will fall into the jar and die.

- Can be used to deter: snails and slugs.

Vegetable Oil and Soy Sauce Trap

An easy trap for earwigs involves pouring vegetable oil and soy sauce into a low dish or saucer and nestling it into the dirt. Another way is using a old sardine tin.

- Can be used to deter: earwigs.

Orange Peel Earwig Trap

Scoop out the insides of orange halves, then leave out in the night. Tip the earwigs collected inside into a bucket of soapy water.

- Can be used to control: earwigs.

Fungicide Spray

This simple fungicide is nothing more than a litre of water into which three teaspoons of bicarb soda and a few drops of dishwashing liquid have been stirred.

Alternatively the bicarb-and-water mixture can be added to a litre of skim milk and seasoned with a pinch of Condy's Crystals.

- Can be used on: fungal diseases such as black spot.

Molasses Spray

Mix together a cup of molasses and a litre of water. Spray on leaves that need protecting. Molasses and water can also be mixed in a ratio one part molasses to four parts water to pour on soil affected by nematodes. Use five litres of mixture for each three square metres.

- Can be used to deter: grasshoppers, caterpillars, nematodes and possums.

Garlic Pesticide

Mix a crushed bulb of garlic with vegetable oil and let stand for two days. Strain off the liquid then add several drops of dishwashing soap. Use a tiny amount of this concentrate in a spray - one millilitre to one litre of water.

- Used to control insect pests. Also has fungicidal properties.

Salt and Vinegar Weedkiller
Mix a cup of salt into a litre of vinegar and brush onto the leaves of any weed you want to kill. Be careful not to spill on any plant you want to keep, or on grass.

- Can be used to control weeds.

Yeast Spray
Mix a teaspoon of yeast-based sandwich spread (such as Vegemite) with water.

- This mixture will attract lacewings and other beneficial predators to the garden.

Homemade Bordeaux Mixture
Take 100g of builders' lime and mix with five litres of water in a plastic bucket until it is dissolved. Take another bucket and dissolve 100g of copper sulfate with the same amount of water. Then take the bucket of lime and (keeping it agitated) pour it into the bucket of copper sulfate. Use the mix within a few days. Spray on the dormant branches of stonefruit trees and raspberry canes. Keep the mixture agitated while spraying.

- Used to control fungal diseases such as curly leaf.

Homemade Burgundy Mixture
Use the same technique as for Bordeaux Mixture, but instead of using lime use washing soda. This mixture is caustic so don't ever spray it on trees when they're in leaf.

- Used to control fungal diseases such as curly leaf.

Milk Fungicide
Organic milk is a natural fungicide and antibiotic. Create a spray by mixing it with water at the ratio 1:10 (not any more as too much milk can encourage the growth of sooty mold). Cover all parts of the plant - stems and both sides of the leaves. Use this spray as a preventative measure, not a cure. This is most effective on soft leaf vegetables.

- Can be used to control fungal diseases such as mildew.

Bicarbonate Fungicide
Mix two litres of water with four tablespoons of bicarbonate of soda, with a drop of detergent and a drop of vegetable oil. The alkaline spray inhibits the growth of fungal spores on leaf surfaces.

- Used to control fungal diseases.

Vinegar Algae Killer
Mix white wine vinegar with water at the ratio 1:3 for a simple non-toxic algae killer.

- Used to control algae.

Homemade Lime Sulfur

Lime sulfur spray can be used as a fungicide and insect deterrent. It can be bought commercially, but if you are willing to go to some effort you may create your own mixture.

Start with an open, well-ventilated outdoor area in which to cook the lime and sulfur. Be warned that sulfur has a foul 'rotten egg' smell - therefore if you live very close to neighbours or have only a small backyard, it's recommended to simply buy a commercial version. If you decide to go ahead, windy weather is best to blow the fumes away.

Create a small firepit on a patch of level ground and surround it with three concrete blocks in a triangle formation so as to support a cooking pot. Build a fire and place a large steel drum on it with a litre of water. When the water starts to boil add a paste of sulfur mixed with a bit of water. Then add lime and stir well.

Cook the mixture for an hour or two, until the ingredients are fully dissolved and the water has turned a dark reddish-brown. Keep adding water to replace that which is evaporated. Let the fire go out naturally then place a cover on the pot as it cools to prevent insects and dust from getting in.

Pour the liquid concentrate through a funnel lined with cheesecloth into several glass jugs. Seal the jugs and use diluted as a spray. The amount of water to be added depends on the season and the type of plants the spray is used on. Seek expert advice if unsure. When mixing the concentrate, use rubber gloves and face mask.

For dormant spraying: Spray fruit trees as the leaf buds swell. Measure and mix two tablespoons of concentrate for each litre of water.

For summer spraying: Use a teaspoon of concentrate to each litre of water and cover all leaves thoroughly with the solution when using as a summer fungicide.

- Can be used against: insects and fungal diseases like mildew and apple scab.

Do not apply within 30 days of using an oil spray as the chemical reaction will cause toxicity.

Disposal of Lime Sulfur Spray
Since lime sulfur is a potentially dangerous chemical mixture, contact your nearest waste disposal authority or environmental protection organisation to ask what their regulations or guidelines are for the disposal of lime sulfur.

Never pour mixed lime sulfur spray down the drain or toilet. It can seriously contaminate waterways and harm the environment. Dispose of empty spray bottles by wrapping them in paper, placing them sealed plastic bags and putting them in the trash.

SPRAYING EQUIPMENT

Any clean spray bottle or garden sprayer will work well for applying your homemade remedies. Make sure the container has never been used for herbicides or other chemicals toxic to plants.

USAGE

It is important to spray organic insecticides directly on pests, saturating them thoroughly. Spray every part of the plant, paying particular attention to leaf joints and the undersides of leaves where pests hide and lay eggs.

With insecticidal soap sprays, once the soap residue has dried on the plant, they will lose their efficacy. Rinse the plant with a spray of clean water and reapply once a week until all signs of infestation have vanished.

COMMERCIAL ORGANIC REMEDIES

Plant Based Organic Insecticides

Neem

Neem is a favourite among organic gardeners as it is relatively non-toxic. It derives from the Indian tree that bears its name, and has a four thousand year history of medicinal and insecticidal use in India and Africa.

Neem is often used to control moths, leaf miners, thrips, whiteflies, caterpillars and mealybugs.

It is commonly sold under the trade name Eco-neem®.

Pyrethrum/Pyrethrins

Pyrethrum spray is the most popular of all the botanical insecticides as it is non-toxic to mammals.

The active ingredient, pyrethrin, is an extract of the Dalmation Daisy (*Tanacetum cinerariifolium*). At low concentrations it irritates and 'knocks down' insects. This fast-acting nature is one of the great advantages to pyrethrum - however insects often recover from short doses of pyrethrin, even if they have been knocked down.

Although pyrethrum is therefore not the most effective in killing insects, it is very useful as a 'flushing agent' that forces an insect to reveal itself from a hiding place (like a crack in bark or in grass).

Pyrethrum breaks down rapidly in sunlight, but you should be careful to protect beneficial insects from exposure. When using pyrethrum to control flying insects, spray it early in the morning and then cover the treated plants with an old bed-sheet or similar large piece of fabric, to exclude bees and other 'good bugs' for 24 hours.

Do not use pyrethrum on plantings where ladybeetles, honeybees and other good bugs can be seen. Used without care, pyrethrum can annihilate these useful garden predators, making *more* work for you.

Mineral-Based Organic Pesticides
Sulfur
Sulfur ranks with neem as one of the oldest pesticides in history. It may be used in a multitude of forms - as a dust, powder to be mixed with water, paste or a liquid. It is effective against fungal infections (such as powdery mildews, leaf blights, fruit rots and rusts) - as well as against spider mites, thrips and psyllids - and is approved for use on fruit and vegetable crops.

Important to bear in mind is the fact that sulfur can harm plants in hot weather - and if used within 20-30 days of any spray oil - can cause phytotoxicity in the plants. Although it is non-toxic to mammals, care should still be taken when handling it as it can irritate skin and eyes.

Lime Sulfur
Most often seen in an orange liquid state, lime sulfur is often sprayed on dormant fruit trees to prevent or control anthroacnose, powdery mildew and other fungi, as well as some insect pests like scales, erophyid mites and thrips. It is foul-smelling and caustic, and can harm plants if applied in hot temperatures. It can also burn leaves, and if used after the green-tip period in spring, it can restrict plant growth and the yield for the year.

How to apply Lime Sulfur
The concentration of lime sulfur solution varies on the type of plant being sprayed.

- Stonefruit - mix 50ml in each litre of water, and spray during the dormant period before bud-swell.
- Pome fruit (apples and pears) - mix 50ml to each litre of water. Do not spray after spring's late green-tip period, as it can restrict plant growth and the yield for the year. Avoid spraying Delicious or Cox's Orange Pippin.
- Grape vines - In NSW, Queensland or the ACT, use 50ml/l ratio. In the rest of Australia, use 100ml/l. Spray just before the leaf-buds burst.
- Citrus - mix between 25ml and 65ml per litre, depending on the type of insect. Spray during summer, onto wet leaves.
- Tomatoes and vegetables - apply 10ml/l and spray all leaves in autumn.

Bordeaux Mixture
Bordeaux mixture is not strictly an organic pesticide, although it is naturally based. It is a combination of lime and copper sulfate and is used to control fungi such as downy mildew, anthracnose, bacterial leaf spot and blight - as well as acting as an insect-repellent.
As with the sulfurs, Bordeaux mix can be phytotoxic and may burn leaves if applied in wet, cool conditions.

ORGANIC PESTICIDE ENHANCER

Piperonyl butoxide is an organic compound used as a component of pesticide formulations. It is a 'synergist', which means that despite having no pesticidal properties of its own, it boosts the potency of certain pesticides, including pyrethrins. It is a obtained from sassafras plants.

Trade Names of Some Organic Remedies

Caterpillar Control
- Dipel (contains Bacillus thuringiensis)
- EcoGrub (contains eucalyptus and tea tree oil)
- Insect Hotel (housing and shelter for beneficial insects)
- Success (contains spinosad, which is derived from naturally occurring beneficial soil bacteria.)

Cockroach Control
- Dead End Mats (recycled cardboard impregnated with a synthetic pyrethrum)
- Orange Guard Crawling Insect Spray (the active ingredient is D-Limonene, a citrus peel extract.)
- Roach Prufe (boric acid)
- Lo-line Sticky Cockroach Trap

Codling Moth Control
- Fruit Tree Grease Bands
- Tanglefoot Pest Barrier
- Trappit™ Barrier Glue
- Biobest sticky trap rolls
- Bug-Scan® sticky and roller traps
- Apple Pouch (nylon 'sockette')
- Codling Moth Trap (pheromone lure)

Deterrent: Bird, Flying Fox and Possum
- Bird Scare Flash Tape

Fruit Fly Control
- Cera Trap
- Naturalure Fruit Fly Attractant
- Eco-Lure Queensland Fruit Fly Trap
- Wild May Fruit Fly Attractant and Trap

Diatomaceous Earth
Products containing diatomaceous earth include:
- Absorbacide
- Organics Made Easy Diatomaceous Earth for Animals
- Amgrow Tomato and Vegetable Dust

Diatomaceous earth is a naturally occurring rock sourced from the fossilised remains of freshwater single-celled plants. It crumbles easily into a pale, fine powder.

This substance can kill insects by absorbing their waxy, oily, outer layer. When this waterproof layer is damaged, the insect or insect egg loses water and dies.

The tiny particles in diatomaceous earth also have microscopically razor sharp edges, which work like sandpaper to abrade and kill the insects. Diatomaceous earth is sometimes called 'sharp sand'.

Internationally diatomaceous earth is included in products which are registered, marketed and certified for the control of cockroaches, silverfish, ants, fleas, flies, ticks, lice, earwigs, aphids, white fly, beetles, loopers, mites, snails, slugs, leaf hoppers. However it is not yet registered for these uses in Australia.

General Purpose Organic Control
- Richgro Beat-A-Bug Insect Spray (contains garlic, chilli, pyrethrins and piperonyl butoxide).
- Eco-Oil (contains canola oil, eucalyptus oil, melaleuca oil and surfactants.)
- Insect Hotel (housing and shelter for beneficial insects)
- Natrasoap (a soap spray made from potassium derived from vegetable oils)
- Orange Guard Crawling Insect Spray (the active ingredient is D-Limonene, a citrus peel extract.)

Exclusion
- Green Harvest Build-A-Frame (support frame for exclusion fabric)
- Green Harvest Cloth Fruit Bags (calico drawstring bags)
- Green Harvest Easy Tunnel
- Green Harvest PestGuard Bags
- PlantGuard Exclusion Fabric

Fungal Control
- Richgro Beat-A-Bug Happy Roses (contains ginseng, garlic oil, vegetable oils, citronella)
- OCP Eco-fungicide (contains potassium bicarbonate)
- Ecocarb (contains potassium bicarbonate)
- Amgrow Lime Sulfur
- Kocide® 3000

Citrus Care
- Eco-Oil (contains canola oil, eucalyptus oil, melaleuca oil and surfactants.)
- Tanglefoot Horticultural Glue
- Green Harvest Tree Wrap (a slightly elastic horticultural clear tape).

Horticultural Glues
- On-Guard Grease Bands
- Tanglefoot Pest Barrier
- Tangle-Trap Insect Trap Coating
- Trappit™ Barrier Glue
- Green Harvest Tree Wrap
- Green Harvest Yellow Sticky Roll Trap

Neem
- Eco-Neem

Pyrethrum
- Kendon Pyrethrum Insect Dust
- Kendon Pyrethrum Insect Killer
- Kendon Pyrethrum Prof. Concentrate
- Yates Pyrethrum Insect Pest Killer

Slug and Snail Control
- Escar-Go
- Multiguard Snail and Slug Pellets
- On-Guard Slug and Snail Trap
- Slugga Copper Barrier Tape

Sticky Garden Traps
- Seabright Laboratories Sticky Thrip Leafminer Trap
- Isca Technologies Citrus Leafminer Trap
- Insectrap
- Trappit Yellow Card Trap
- Green Harvest Yellow Sticky Roll Trap

Wasp Control
- Envirosafe European Wasp Catcher

Weed Control
- Weed Blitz Organic Herbicide

FRUIT CARE ALMANAC - WINTER

Here is a handy reference guide for care of fruiting plants throughout the year.

EARLY WINTER

*Circa June (southern hemisphere) and
December (northern hemisphere)*

Raspberries
- Raspberries can be planted any time from late fall up until early spring before new growth begins.

Stonefruit
- Feed stonefruit monthly, using either seaweed or a flower and fruit fertilizer.
- Spray with Bordeaux or lime sulfur in autumn/early winter as leaves fall, then again in winter as the flower buds swell. This controls brown rot, leaf curl, scale, mite, aphids and mealybug.

Plums
- Do *not* prune in the fall, or cold-weather injury or infection may set in.
- Keep an eye on the lower bark and branches for mice or rabbit injury. If this is a problem, you may need to install tree guards or fence in young trees with chicken wire for the winter.
- Once young trees are established, they need to be fertilized all year long for good crop yields. However, cut back the nitrogen in fall and winter to avoid encouraging new growth in those seasons.

Bananas
- If your bananas are in tropical or sub-tropical zones, keep the soil moist and continue to feed bananas once a month.
- In temperate or cool zones, create a warm microclimate for your banana plants. Plant them in terracotta pots near a ma-

sonry wall that faces the sun. (North-facing in the southern hemisphere, south-facing in the northern hemisphere.)
- If possible, plant at the top of a gentle slope. Frost tends to settle in low places.
- Remove a few of the lower leaves. This will encourage the banana plant to gow taller, so that if there is a frost, it will pass underneath.
- Scrape away the mulch from the base of the plant. This did its job over the fall period, trapping the last of the summer heat, but now is the time to replace it with a generous dose of compost. Organic matter will break down and generate heat. Level out the compost by raking it.
- Keep your banana plant well irrigated and give it regular doses of liquid seaweed throughout the coming winter.
- Build a hessian/burlap frost barrier around the plants in early winter. This consists of an upright wire fence encircling the plant, covered with hessian/burlap. You can stuff the lower part of this wire/burlap cage with clean straw as an extra frost protectant.
- Put a temporary a lid on top to protect the plant's topmost leaves during winter frosts.

Dragonfruit and Other Fruiting Cactus
- Monitor your plants for rot.
- Reduce watering.

Citrus
- Apply nitrogenous fertilizers (such as composted poultry manure) several weeks before your mature citrus trees flower; that is, in early- to mid-winter for warmer coastal areas, or in late winter for cooler inland districts. In sandy soils, which are easily leached, split the dressing into two applications — two-thirds in late winter, with the rest applied in the period from spring to summer.

MIDWINTER

*Circa July (southern hemisphere) and
January (northern hemisphere)*

Raspberries
- These can be planted any time from late fall up until early spring before new growth begins.

Bananas
- Keep the soil moist especially during the dry times.
- Maintain a 3- to 4-inch (8-10cm) mulch layer over the root systems.

Stonefruit
- Feed monthly using either liquid seaweed or a potassium-rich, organic fertilizer such as granite meal, kelp meal or greensand.

Dragonfruit and Other Fruiting Cactus
- Monitor your plants for rot, which is more common in cold weather.
- Keep watering at a minimum.

Stonefruit
- Spray with Bordeaux mixture or lime sulfur in winter as the flower buds swell. This controls brown rot, leaf curl, scale, mite, aphids and mealybug.

Plums
- Do not prune in the fall or winter, or cold-weather injury or infection may occur.
- Once young trees are established, they need regular fertilizing all year long for good crop yields. Reduce nitrogenous fertilizers in fall and winter to avoid encouraging new growth in those seasons.

- Keep an eye on the lower bark and branches for mice or rabbit injury; if this could be a problem, you may need to install tree guards or fence in young trees with chicken wire for the winter.

Citrus
- Any established citrus trees that may have become infected with melanose disease or brown rot disease need winter care. Remove old mulch and fallen fruit. Discard this waste by hot-composting or sealing it firmly in a plastic bag and putting it on the rubbish bin. It will be contaminated with fungal disease. Pull out weeds from the base of the trees. Spread fresh, clean mulch around your trees, ensuring that you keep the mulch from touching the trunk. Fresh mulch reduces the risk of fungal spores being splashed by rain (or irrigation) onto healthy citrus leaves. Spray infected trees thoroughly with cupric hydroxide. Make certain all parts of the trees are well soaked, especially leaf undersides, bark and any cracks in the bark.
- Winter is the time to control any stink bugs, such as bronze orange bugs or spined citrus bugs on your citrus trees. Spray trees twice in mid-winter with horticultural oil, to smother the nymphal stages of the bugs. This will reduce the number that reach adulthood.
- Feed citrus trees with a potassium-rich, organic fertilizer such as granite meal, kelp meal or greensand.
- In warm, dry regions, water citrus regularly, especially in windy weather, but do not feed them until after they finish flowering. Too much nitrogen encourages citrus to drop their fruit. It also boosts the lush, leafy growth that attracts destructive aphids.

Figs
- Control snails.

LATE WINTER

Circa August (southern hemisphere) and February (northern hemisphere)

Raspberries
- These can be planted any time from late fall up until early spring before new growth begins.

Bananas
- Keep the soil moist.
- Maintain a 3- to 4-inch (8-10cm) mulch layer over the root systems.

Currants and Gooseberries
- In late winter, fertilize with compost or aged manure.
- Annual pruning in late winter will help boost the berry yield and the looks of your shrub. Prune out broken or drooping branches.
- Watch out for powdery mildew, a white fungus that coats leaves and can develop on the fruits too. Cut off and remove infected portions of the plant.
- If powdery mildew is a serious problem, consider purchasing certified disease-free varieties and plant them further apart to encourage plenty of air movement between bushes to encourage healthy growth.

Dragonfruit and Other Fruiting Cactus
- Continue to monitor for rot and give minimal irrigation.

Apples and Pears
- Apply horticultural white oil (see the chapter on 'Pest and Disease Remedies') before buds swell, to control any mites or scale that have appeared on your trees. When European red mite numbers are high, the bright red eggs show up on

smaller branches and twigs. Oil smothers their overwintering eggs. Spray it when temperature is above 40 degrees Fahrenheit (4 degrees Celsius).

Stonefruit
- Feed monthly using either seaweed or an organic flower and fruit fertilizer. Do not use a high nitrogen fertlizer in cooler seasons.
- Spray with Bordeaux or lime sulfur in winter as the flower buds swell. This controls brown rot, leaf curl, scale, mite, aphids and mealybug.
- Do not prune in winter because there is a greater risk of infection.
- Keep an eye on the lower bark and branches for mouse or rabbit injury; if this could be a problem, you may need to install tree guards or fence in young trees with chicken wire for the winter.

Berries
- Monitor berry-bearing plants for botrytis rot, also known as gray mold of strawberry and raspberry. Your plants should already be pruned and trained in an open shape that encourages good air circulation, which can reduce fungal infections.

Citrus
- You will only need to apply citrus scab control sprays if the disease has caused problems in previous seasons. If you see symptoms of citrus scab, use a copper fungicide to prevent infection on new growth and young fruit. You might have to apply additional sprays at monthly intervals to prevent infection of new flushes or foliage or swelling fruit.
- Aphids may attack new growth of young trees. If you find them on your trees, thoroughly spray with horticultural oil or insecticidal soap. Aphid control on mature trees is not

usually needed because damage is not usually bad enough to warrant spraying.
- For citrus leafminers (on new growth), spray horticultural oil twice, spaced two weeks apart, only when new flush is present. This will protect the new growth.
- On cooler inland districts, apply nitrogenous fertilizers (such as composted poultry manure) several weeks before your citrus trees flower. In sandy soils, which are easily leached, split the dressing into two applications — two-thirds in late winter, with the rest applied in the period from spring to summer.
- For young citrus trees (less than five years old), fertilize only three to four times per year: early spring, mid spring and early summer.

Figs
- Prune your fig trees lightly, aiming for good branch structure and size.
- Control snails.

FRUIT CARE ALMANAC
- SPRING

EARLY SPRING

Circa September (southern hemisphere) and March (northern hemisphere)

Bananas
- Keep the soil moist especially during periods of low rainfall.
- Maintain a 3- to 4-inch (8-10cm) mulch layer over the root systems.
- Bananas requite regular fertilizing. Apply an organic fertilizer once each month throughout spring and early summer to boost growth and productivity.

Stonefruit
- As buds are swelling, spray the trees with a copper-based fungicide to control curly-leaf disease.
- Feed your stonefruit trees after flowering finishes, using a complete organic fertilizer.
- Prune in early spring or mid-summer to avoid infection. The best time for pruning is usually spring for young trees and mid-summer for established ones.

Berries
- Raspberries and blackberries can be planted any time from late fall up until early spring before new growth begins.
- A three-spray organic fungicide program (just before bloom, full bloom, petal fall) may eliminate the need for fungicides during harvest. *Bacillus subtilis* is one such registered organic fungicide.
- Raspberry plants should not be allowed to dry out during their flowering and fruiting period.
- Raspberries should be fed in early spring with an all-purpose organic fertilizer.

Pear, Quince and Cherry.
- Spraying pear, quince and cherry trees with lime first in spring and again in mid-summer is an effective control measure for pear and cherry slug The use of too much lime, however, should be avoided since it alters the pH of the soil beneath the trees. *Bacillus thuringiensis* (Bt) is a biological control that can be sprayed to naturally control pear and cherry slug. Spinosad is another organic insecticide. It is based on chemical compounds found in the bacterial species *Saccharopolyspora spinosa*. Yates 'Success' contains spinosad and can be sprayed to control pear and cherry slug.

Dragonfruit and Other Fruiting Cactus
- Monitor for rot and keep irrigation low.

Pawpaw
- For best fruiting, apply liquid potash every 2 to 3 weeks, starting before the formation of flower buds and continuing through to the end of fruit production. Pawpaws are heavy feeders, so for best fruit yield apply a potassium-rich, organic fertilizer such as granite meal, kelp meal or greensand throughout the growing season.
- Keep pawpaw plants moist but well-drained. If rainfall is low, water them at least twice a week throughout the growing season - i.e. spring and summer.

Berries
- A three-spray organic fungicide program (just before bloom, full bloom, petal fall) may eliminate the need for fungicides during harvest.
- Raspberry plants should not be allowed to dry out during their flowering and fruiting period.

Citrus

- For rust mites and spider mites, apply horticultural oil or a general miticide registered for citrus.

- After blossoming, when around two-thirds of the petals have fallen, you can apply a post-blossom fertilizing spray containing copper, zinc and manganese. The copper in the nutritional spray acts as the second spray for citrus scab and will also help control melanose. If you do not use a fertilizing spray, use another organic product containing copper fungicide registered for use on citrus scab.

- *Note:* Never mix any products containing oil and sulfur. Wait three weeks between applying products containing oil and sulfur.

- Phosphorus and potassium for citrus: Timing not as vital for feeding citrus trees with phosphate or potassium fertilizer than it is for nitrogen fertilizer. Phosphate and potassium don't leach out of the soil as easily as nitrogen, Besides, they take between three months and three years to be absorbed into the tree. Apply a potassium-rich, organic fertilizer such as granite meal, kelp meal or greensand in early spring. This allows time for the phosphate to be absorbed before the period of most rapid growth. Trees need to have fertilizers spread within reach of their root systems. Spread the fertilizers on the soil surface in a strip or band under the edge of the leaf canopy. Roots generally extend out as far as the edge of the tree's leaf canopy, or 'dripline'.

MID SPRING

*Circa October (southern hemisphere) and
April (northern hemisphere)*

Bananas
- Keep the soil moist but well-drained.
- Protect bananas from strong winds.
- Maintain a 3-4 inch (8-10cm) mulch layer over banana root systems.
- Spread a general organic fertilizer once a month during the period of most rapid growth to boost fruiting.

Citrus
- Apply a potassium-rich, organic fertilizer such as granite meal, kelp meal or greensand this month, as for last month. Citrus trees are heavy feeders. Spread the fertilizers on the soil in a circular strip or band under the edge of the leaf canopy.

Avocados
- Feed with a potassium-rich, organic fertilizer such as granite meal, kelp meal or greensand.

Pawpaws
- For best fruiting, apply liquid potash every 2 to 3 weeks, starting before the formation of flower buds and continuing through to the end of fruit production. Pawpaws are heavy feeders, so for best fruit yield apply a potassium-rich, organic fertilizer such as granite meal, kelp meal or greensand throughout the growing season.
- Keep pawpaw plants moist but well-drained. If rainfall is low, water them at least twice a week throughout the growing season - i.e. spring and summer.

Dragonfruit and Other Fruiting Cactus
- Continue to monitor for rot.
- If plants are in a hothouse, gradually begin to increase the amount of irrigation as the weather warms up.

Grapes
- Most grape diseases can be largely prevented with careful trellising and pruning (for good ventilation) and mulching.
- If you see symptoms of powdery mildew (evidenced by whitish patches on leaves) use preventive sprays made of one part milk to five parts water, mixed together well and sprayed over the entire plant, to minimize the problem.
- Mulch grape vines to deter vine borer moth.

Raspberries and other Berries
- Keep berry plants moist during their flowering and fruiting seasons.

Stonefruit
- Feed stonefruit trees every month during the growing season, using either seaweed or a potassium-rich, organic fertilizer such as granite meal, kelp meal or greensand.

- Fruit fly management: In some regions there may be a legal responsibility to bait and spray fruit fly. Bait male fruit flies with fruit fly attractants such as 'Dak pots'. If your trees are growing in a temperate zone and are early fruiting varieties, their fruit may ripen enough to harvest before peak fruit fly season. Harvest fully formed fruit as soon as they develop some fragrance and the flesh has softened a little. Clean up fallen or spoiled fruit and either bury it at least 50cm deep or dispose of it in sealed plastic bags in your rubbish bin. Do not compost fruit that is infested with fruit fly.

- European wasps are attracted to ripe fruit. If you locate their nests, call in professionals to remove them.

- Use close-woven netting to protect fruit from birds and fruitbats. Open-weave standard half-inch (1cm) square bird netting can injure or kill birds.

Apples and Pears
- Look for symptoms of mites or scale. To control these, wait until your apple or pear trees show their first shoots. Apply the appropriate horticultural oil sprays when new green leaves are 0.25 to 0.5 inch (1/2 - 1cm) - long. If you wait until this stage to spray with oil, you might get even better control of scale than if you spray earlier. Also, the eggs of European red mite start to hatch at this time. Always spray horticultural oil at temperatures above 5 degrees Celsius (40 degrees Fahrenheit), and do not apply it within fourteen days before or after using sulfur.
- Look for symptoms of aphids. To control these, wait until your apple or pear trees show their first shoots. Apply the appropriate sprays when new green leaves are 0.25 to 0.5 inch (1/2 - 1cm) - long. You can also spray when blossom buds have appeared but are not yet open. Use neem or insecticidal soap. For insecticidal soap, repeat application 3 to 4 days later.

- During the period when apples and pears are in blossom, do not use insecticides. Save the bees.

- Look for any symptoms of scab. Apply the appropriate organic fungicide sprays when new green leaves are 0.25 to 0.5 inch (1/2 - 1cm) - long. Use copper spray, Bordeaux mixture, Kocide® 300, sulfur or any other organic fungus remedies listed in this book.

- Look for symptoms of powdery mildew. Spray when blossom buds have appeared but are not yet open. The remedy is lime sulfur or sulfur.

LATE SPRING

Circa November (southern hemisphere) and May (northern hemisphere)

Bananas
- Keep the soil moist but well-drained.
- Protect bananas from strong winds.
- Maintain a 3-4 inch (8-10cm) mulch layer over banana root systems.
- Spread a general organic fertilizer once a month during the period of most rapid growth to boost fruiting.

Berries
- Fruiting plants with berry crops must not be allowed to dry out during their flowering and fruiting seasons.

Pawpaws
- For best fruiting, apply liquid potash every 2 to 3 weeks, starting before the formation of flower buds and continuing through to the end of fruit production. Pawpaws are heavy feeders, so for best fruit yield apply a potassium-rich, organic fertilizer such as granite meal, kelp meal or greensand throughout the growing season.
- Keep pawpaw plants moist but well-drained. If rainfall is low, water them at least twice a week throughout the growing season - i.e. spring and summer.

Citrus

- Whiteflies and scale may bring sooty mold. Their excretions of honey dew drip onto the leaves or fruit below their feeding areas. A black, soot-like mold grows on the honeydew's surface. Control the insects by spraying with horticultural oil or insecticidal soap and the sooty mold will eventually disappear.

- Fertilize older citrus trees (ones that were planted over five years ago) using either liquid seaweed or a potassium-rich, organic fertilizer such as granite meal, kelp meal or greensand.

Stonefruit

- Feed stonefruit trees every month during the growing season, using either seaweed or a potassium-rich, organic fertilizer such as granite meal, kelp meal or greensand.

- Fruit fly management: In some regions there may be a legal responsibility to bait and spray fruit fly. Bait male fruit flies with fruit fly attractants such as 'Dak pots'. If your trees are growing in a temperate zone and are early fruiting varieties, their fruit may ripen enough to harvest before peak fruit fly season. Harvest fully formed fruit as soon as they develop some fragrance and the flesh has softened a little. Clean up fallen or spoiled fruit and either bury it at least 50cm deep or dispose of it in sealed plastic bags in your rubbish bin. Do not compost fruit that is infested with fruit fly.

- European wasps are attracted to ripe fruit. If you locate their nests, call in professionals to remove them.

- Use close-woven netting to protect fruit from birds and fruit-bats. This also guards against fruit fly. Open-weave standard half-inch (1cm) square bird netting can injure or kill birds.

Apples and Pears
- Look for symptoms of codling moth. Spray trees with one of the appropriate organic insecticides listed in this book, such as spinosad. Spraying at this time is critical for first-generation codling moth control.

- Look for symptoms of aphids. To control these, spray with neem or insecticidal soap. For insecticidal soap, repeat application 3 to 4 days later.

- Look for symptoms of powdery mildew, fruit rot or scab. Spray with lime sulfur, sulfur or any of the appropriate organic fungicides listed in this book. Apply 10 days after petal-fall and at 10-day intervals through late spring. Discontinue sulfur use when temperatures reach 90 degrees Fahrenheit (5 degrees Celsius).

- Look for symptoms of mites. Severe mite feeding results in brown foliage that eventually becomes bronzed. Apply horticultural oil, or neem, or insecticidal soap 10 days after petal-fall and at 10-day intervals throughout late spring. For insecticidal soap repeat application 2 to 3 days later.

- To prevent damage to foliage or fruits, never use a horticultural oil with any sulfur-containing remedies. Allow at least 14 days between applications of sulfur-containing compounds and the use of a summer oil. Apply oil at temperatures above 40 degrees Fahrenheit (5 degrees Celsius) and below 90 degrees Fahrenheit (35 degrees Celsius).

- Look for symptoms of scale. Spray with horticultural oil or insecticidal soap. Apply 10 days after petal-fall and at 10-day intervals through late spring. For insecticidal soap repeat application 2 to 3 days later.

FRUIT CARE ALMANAC
- SUMMER

EARLY SUMMER

*Circa December (southern hemisphere) and
June (northern hemisphere)*

All Fruiting Plants
- Mulch all trees, shrubs and other fruit-bearing plants.
- Ensure that all fruiting plants are well-watered as the weather warms up.

Currants and Gooseberries
- Add an organic mulch, such as straw, in early summer to help keep roots cool and soil moist.

Stonefruit
- Spray stonefruit again with an organic copper-based fungicide when fruits are nearly mature. Read the label and make sure you observe the manufacturer's withholding period between spraying and harvesting.
- At this time of year it might be necessary to thin out your fruit by picking off a few here and there to make sure your fruit quality is good (leave the biggest and healthiest on the tree) and to avoid breaking branches because of over-heavy bunches of fruit.

Dragonfruit and Other Fruiting Cactus
- Prune during the growing period summer- autumn. While plants are actively growing their wounds heal more rapidly and are less likely to rot.
- Water dragonfruit and cactus well in summer. Feed them monthly with either liquid seaweed or a potassium-rich, organic fertilizer such as granite meal, kelp meal or greensand.

Pear, Quince and Cherry.
- Spraying pear, quince and cherry trees with lime first in spring and again in mid-summer is an effective control measure for pear and cherry slug The use of too much lime, however, should be avoided since it alters the pH of the soil beneath the trees. *Bacillus thuringiensis* (Bt) is a biological control that can be sprayed to naturally control pear and cherry slug. Yates 'Success' contains spinosad and can also be sprayed to control pear and cherry slug.

Guavas
- Feed them monthly during the summer with either liquid seaweed or a potassium-rich, organic fertilizer such as granite meal, kelp meal or greensand. Simply scatter the fertilizer on the ground and water thoroughly.
- Control weeds and grass with organic mulches.

Pawpaws
- Continue to apply a potassium-rich, organic fertilizer such as granite meal, kelp meal or greensand every 2 to 3 weeks throughout the growing season.

- Keep pawpaw plants moist but well-drained. If rainfall is low, water them at least twice a week throughout the warm-weather growing season.

Bananas
- Keep the soil moist but well-drained.
- Protect banana plants from strong winds.
- Maintain a 3- to 4-inch (8-10cm) mulch layer over banana root systems.
- Spread a general organic fertilizer once a month during the period of most rapid growth to boost fruiting.

Raspberries
- Raspberry plants produce their fruit on canes that sprouted during the previous year. Newly planted summer-bearing raspberries should be left alone for the first year to establish themselves.
- Raspberry plants must not be allowed to dry out during their flowering and fruiting seasons.

Avocados
- Water your avocado regularly during dry spells, keeping the soil moist, but not too wet. Once a month, water them deeply to flush any accumulated salts through the soil.
- Feed monthly with either liquid seaweed or a potassium-rich, organic fertilizer such as granite meal, kelp meal or greensand.

Figs
- Protect fruit from birds, flying foxes etc.
- Water your fig trees regularly but deeply during the growing season. Periodic deep soakings will help leach any salts out of the soil, which will give a better crop. Be careful not to over-water when fruit is ripening, because this can cause fruit to split.

Stonefruit
- Feed monthly using either liquid seaweed or a potassium-rich, organic fertilizer such as granite meal, kelp meal or greensand.

- Fruit fly management: In some regions there may be a legal responsibility to bait and spray fruit fly. Bait male fruit flies with fruit fly attractants such as 'Dak pots'. If your trees are growing in a temperate zone and are early fruiting varieties, their fruit may ripen enough to harvest before peak fruit fly season. Harvest fully formed fruit as soon as they develop some fragrance and the flesh has softened a little. Clean up fallen or spoiled fruit and either bury it at least 50cm deep or dispose of it in sealed plastic bags in your rubbish bin. Do not compost fruit that is infested with fruit fly.

- European wasps are attracted to ripe fruit. If you locate their nests, call in professionals to remove them.

- Use close-woven netting to protect fruit from birds and fruit-bats. This also guards against fruit fly. Open-weave standard half-inch (1cm) square bird netting can injure or kill birds.

- Water your stonefruit trees well when they are in leaf during dry weather. Drip-irrigation is ideal because the water goes straight to the roots without wetting the leaves. Avoid wetting foliage when watering or feeding; water droplets can burn leaves in hot sunlight, or attract fungus overnight.

- Thinning stonefruit by picking some off is important to prevent branches breaking under the weight of the fruit. If branches do break, prune them back into the undamaged wood, preferably cutting back to a natural fork so that you don't leave behind a woody stub.

Citrus
- Apply either liquid seaweed or a potassium-rich, organic fertilizer such as granite meal, kelp meal or greensand.
- Monitor citrus trees for scale, leafminer, sooty mold and any other citrus pests and diseases.
- Keep trees moist and well mulched.

Berries
- Look for symptoms of 'mummyberry of blueberry'. Fruit turn grayish and dry, then drop off before ripening. Pick off any infected fruit before they fall. Clear away weeds and grass. Surround your plants with a thick layer of organic mulch, preferably containing pine needles to slightly acidify the soil.

Apples and Pears
- Look for symptoms of codling moth. Spray trees with one of the appropriate organic insecticides listed in this book, such as spinosad.

- Look for symptoms of aphids. To control these, spray with neem or insecticidal soap. For insecticidal soap, repeat application 3 to 4 days later.
- Look for symptoms of powdery mildew, fruit rot, scab or other fungal diseases. Spray with any of the appropriate organic fungicides listed in this book. Observe manufacturer's instructions for withholding periods between spraying and harvest.

- Look for symptoms of mites. Apply horticultural oil, or neem, or pyrethrins or insecticidal soap. For insecticidal soap repeat application 2 to 3 days later.

- To prevent damage to foliage or fruits, never use a horticultural oil with any sulfur-containing remedies. Allow at least 14 days between applications of sulfur-containing compounds and the use of a summer oil. Apply oil at temperatures above 40 degrees Fahrenheit (5 degrees Celsius) and below 90 degrees Fahrenheit (35 degrees Celsius).

- Look for symptoms of scale. San Jose scale shows up as a conspicuous red spot on the fruit. Apply pesticide when crawlers are active. Spray with horticultural oil or insecticidal soap. For insecticidal soap repeat application 2 to 3 days later.

MIDSUMMER

Circa January (southern hemisphere) and July (northern hemisphere)

All Fruiting Plants
- Mulch all fruiting plants, if not already mulched.
- Keep up the water and make sure roots are moist.

Bananas
- Keep the soil moist but well-drained.
- Protect bananas from strong winds.
- Maintain a 3- to 4-inch (8-10cm) mulch layer over banana root systems.
- Spread a general organic fertilizer once a month during the period of most rapid growth to boost fruiting.

Currants and Gooseberries
- Make sure your plants have sufficient dappled shade. Intense sunlight can burn the leaves.
- If you notice that leaves are small and few, the plant may need more watering.

Avocados
- Water avocados regularly during dry periods, keeping the soil moist, but not overly wet. Once a month, water deeply to flush accumulated salts through the soil.

- Feed monthly either with liquid seaweed or a potassium-rich, organic fertilizer such as granite meal, kelp meal or greensand.

Pawpaws
- Continue to apply a potassium-rich, organic fertilizer such as granite meal, kelp meal or greensand every 2 to 3 weeks throughout the growing season.

- Keep pawpaw plants moist but well-drained. If rainfall is low, water them at least twice a week throughout the warm-weather growing season.

Dragonfruit and Other Fruiting Cactus
- If any pruning is necessary do it during the active growing period summer- autumn, so that wounds will heal more rapidly and rot is less likely.
- Water well in summer and feed monthly with either liquid seaweed or a potassium-rich, organic fertilizer such as granite meal, kelp meal or greensand.

Guavas
- Irrigate slowly and deeply to keep roots moist but not waterlogged. Soakings once or twice a week during the summer should be sufficient.
- Control weeds and grass with organic mulches.
- Pruning should be unnecessary except to remove dead or damaged branches or to thin out branches that overlap with others.
- Feed monthly, using either liquid seaweed or a potassium-rich, organic fertilizer such as granite meal, kelp meal or greensand.

Figs
- Protect fruit from birds, flying foxes, possums etc.
- Water regularly but deeply during the growing season.
- Avoid over-watering when fruit is ripening, because this can cause fruit to split.

Stonefruit
- Feed monthly, using either liquid seaweed or a potassium-rich, organic fertilizer such as granite meal, kelp meal or greensand.

- Fruit fly management: In some regions there may be a legal responsibility to bait and spray fruit fly. Bait male fruit flies with fruit fly attractants such as 'Dak pots'. If your trees are growing in a temperate zone and are early fruiting varieties, their fruit may ripen enough to harvest before peak fruit fly season. Harvest fully formed fruit as soon as they develop some fragrance and the flesh has softened a little. Clean up fallen or spoiled fruit and either bury it at least 50cm deep or dispose of it in sealed plastic bags in your rubbish bin. Do not compost fruit that is infested with fruit fly.

- European wasps are attracted to ripe fruit. If you locate their nests, call in professionals to remove them.

- Use close-woven netting to protect fruit from birds and fruit-bats. This also guards against fruit fly. Open-weave standard half-inch (1cm) square bird netting can injure or kill birds.

- Water your stonefruit trees well when they are in leaf during dry weather. Drip-irrigation is ideal because the water goes straight to the roots without wetting the leaves. Avoid wetting foliage when watering or feeding; water droplets can burn leaves in hot sunlight, or attract fungus overnight.

- Thinning stonefruit by picking some off is important to prevent branches breaking under the weight of the fruit. If branches do break, prune them back into the undamaged wood, preferably cutting back to a natural fork so that you don't leave behind a stub.
- Brown rot of cherry, peach and plum; this fungus overwinters on mummified fruit hanging on the tree or lying on the ground. Clean up fallen fruit before, during and after harvest. Remove and destroy all unharvested fruit and mummified fruit from trees after harvest.

Berries
- Look for symptoms of 'mummyberry of blueberry'. Fruit turn grayish and dry, then drop off before ripening. Pick off any infected fruit before they fall. Clear away weeds and grass. Surround your plants with a thick layer of organic mulch, preferably containing pine needles to slightly acidify the soil.

LATE SUMMER

Circa February (southern hemisphere) and August (northern hemisphere

Bananas
- Keep the soil moist but well-drained.
- Protect bananas from strong winds.
- Maintain a thick mulch layer over banana root systems.
- Spread a general organic fertilizer once a month during the period of most rapid growth to boost fruiting.

Avocados
- Water avocados regularly during dry periods, keeping the soil moist, but not overly wet. Once a month, water deeply to flush accumulated salts through the soil.

- Feed monthly either with liquid seaweed or a potassium-rich, organic fertilizer such as granite meal, kelp meal or greensand.

Raspberries
- These plants must not be allowed to dry out during their flowering and fruiting seasons.
- Pruning: Raspberry plants produce their fruit on canes that sprouted during the previous year. Newly planted summer bearing raspberries should be left alone for the first year to establish themselves.
- For established plants: After fruiting, the canes should be cut back to the ground, after which new second year canes will begin to develop around the crown of the plant. Remove all but the strongest 7-10 canes and attach the remaining canes to the top wire. Before new growth begins in the following spring, cut the canes back to 5 feet (150cm) to induce lateral branching.

Dragonfruit and Other Fruiting Cactus
- If any pruning is necessary do it during the active growing period summer- autumn, so that wounds will heal more rapidly and rot is less likely.
- Water well in summer and feed monthly with either liquid seaweed or a potassium-rich, organic fertilizer such as granite meal, kelp meal or greensand.

Grapes
- These fruits are a favorite food of many wild birds. Protect your grapes with close-woven netting.

Pawpaws
- Continue to apply a potassium-rich, organic fertilizer such as granite meal, kelp meal or greensand every 2 to 3 weeks throughout the growing season.

- Keep pawpaw plants moist but well-drained. If rainfall is low, water them at least twice a week throughout the warm-weather growing season.

Guavas
- Irrigate slowly and deeply to keep roots moist but not waterlogged. Weekly to twice-weekly soakings during the summer should be sufficient.
- Control weeds and grass with organic mulches.
- Pruning should be unnecessary except to remove dead or damaged branches or to thin out branches that overlap with others.
- Feed monthly, using either liquid seaweed or a potassium-rich, organic fertilizer such as granite meal, kelp meal or greensand.

Figs
- Protect fruit from birds, flying foxes, possums etc.
- Water regularly but deeply during the growing season.
- Avoid over-watering when fruit is ripening, because this can cause fruit to split.

Stonefruit
- Feed monthly, using either liquid seaweed or a potassium-rich, organic fertilizer such as granite meal, kelp meal or greensand.

- Fruit fly management: In some regions there may be a legal responsibility to bait and spray fruit fly. Bait male fruit flies with fruit fly attractants such as 'Dak pots'. If your trees are growing in a temperate zone and are early fruiting varieties, their fruit may ripen enough to harvest before peak fruit fly season. Harvest fully formed fruit as soon as they develop some fragrance and the flesh has softened a little. Clean up fallen or spoiled fruit and either bury it at least 50cm deep or dispose of it in sealed plastic bags in your rubbish bin. Do not compost fruit that is infested with fruit fly.

- European wasps are attracted to ripe fruit. If you locate their nests, call in professionals to remove them.

- Use close-woven netting to protect fruit from birds and fruit-bats. This also guards against fruit fly. Open-weave standard half-inch (1cm) square bird netting can injure or kill birds.

- Water your stonefruit trees well when they are in leaf during dry weather. Drip-irrigation is ideal because the water goes straight to the roots without wetting the leaves. Avoid wetting foliage when watering or feeding; water droplets can burn leaves in hot sunlight, or attract fungus overnight.

- Thinning stonefruit by picking some off is important to prevent branches breaking under the weight of the fruit. If branches do break, prune them back into the undamaged wood, preferably cutting back to a natural fork so that you don't leave behind a stub.

- Pruning: In late summer or fall after harvesting, prune your stonefruit trees to keep their vase shape. Most stonefruit cultivars naturally form a vase-shaped tree which is a great way to allow sunlight and ventilation into the center of the tree. Using clean, sterilized secateurs, cut off any dead, whippy or crossing branches.

- Brown rot of cherry, peach and plum; this fungus overwinters on mummified fruit hanging on the tree or lying on the ground. Clean up fallen fruit before, during and after harvest. Remove and destroy all unharvested fruit and mummified fruit from trees after harvest.

Citrus

- Inspect citrus trees for mites. If necessary, spray horticultural oil or other organic miticides as listed in this book.
- Apply either liquid seaweed or a potassium-rich, organic fertilizer such as granite meal, kelp meal or greensand.
- Keep trees moist and well mulched.

FRUIT CARE ALMANAC - FALL

EARLY FALL/AUTUMN

*Circa March (southern hemisphere) and
September (northern hemisphere*

Bananas
- Keep the soil moist but well-drained.
- Protect bananas from strong winds.
- Maintain a 3-4 inch (8-10cm) mulch layer over banana root systems.

Avocados
- Keep the soil moist, but not overly wet.

- Feed avocados either with liquid seaweed or a potassium-rich, organic fertilizer such as granite meal, kelp meal or greensand.

Raspberries

- Raspberry plants must not be allowed to dry out during their fruiting seasons.
- For established plants: After harvesting is over the canes that bore fruit should be cut back to the ground. New second-year canes will develop around the crown of the plant. Remove all but the strongest 7-10 canes and attach the remaining canes to the top wire. Before new growth begins in the following spring, cut the canes back to 5 feet (150cm) to induce lateral branching. Never prune off new raspberry canes that haven't produced fruit yet, because they will produce the next year's crop.

Dragonfruit and Other Fruiting Cactus
- If any pruning is necessary do it during the active growing period summer- autumn, so that wounds will heal more rapidly and rot is less likely.
- Keep up the irrigation as long as temperatures remain high and the air is warm. When temperatures drop, cut back the watering.
- Continue to feed with either liquid seaweed or a potassium-rich, organic fertilizer such as granite meal, kelp meal or greensand. Fruit will ripen and become ready to pick from late fall to late winter.

Guavas
- Irrigate slowly and deeply to keep roots moist but not waterlogged. Weekly to biweekly soakings during the summer should be sufficient.
- Control weeds and grass with organic mulches.
- Pruning should be unnecessary except to remove dead or damaged branches or to thin out branches that overlap with others.

Figs
- Protect fruit from birds and other fruit raiders. See the section on 'Birds' in 'General Fruit Pests and Diseases'. If using netting, choose the close-woven type.
- Water figs regularly but deeply when needed, because they are still producing fruit. Avoid over-watering when fruit is ripening, since this can cause fruit to split.

Berries
- Prune berry fruit by removing all old canes of raspberry and bramble bushes.
- Loosely tie together the new canes for next year's crops.
- Prune blackcurrant bushes by cutting out all old, dark coloured branches to leave younger ones.
- Clean up strawberry beds.
- Inspect blueberries for 'mummyberry of blueberry'. Fruit turns grayish, dries up and drops off before ripening. Remove infected
- fruit before they fall. Clear away weeds and debris from your blueberry plants, and mulch with pine needles.

Citrus
- Inspect citrus trees for spider mites. If necessary, spray with horticultural oil. Do not apply when temperature is higher than 94°F (34°C). Do not apply oil within three weeks of any remedy containing sulfur. Do not spray oil after mid-fall/autumn as this may increase the trees' susceptibility to cold damage.
- Apply organic manures in fall/autumn. This allows them time to break down and release the nutrients for spring growth.

Stonefruit
- Spray peach and nectarine trees as leaves fall, with Bordeaux mixture or lime sulfur in autumn as leaves fall. This helps to control brown rot, leaf curl, scale, mite, aphids and mealybug.

- Prune all stonefruit trees as their fruit is harvested. Most stonefruit cultivars naturally form a vase-shaped tree which is a great way to allow sunlight and ventilation into the center of the tree. Prune to keep their vase shape. Using clean, sterilized secateurs, cut off any dead, whippy or crossing branches.

- Apply limestone or dolomite around stonefruit. Feed one last time before winter, either with liquid seaweed or a potassium-rich, organic fertilizer such as granite meal, kelp meal or greensand.

- In the fall, rake away all debris and fallen leaves. Clean up fallen fruit before, during and after harvest. Remove and destroy all unharvested fruit and mummified fruit from trees after harvest.

Apples
- Rake and destroy fallen leaves and fruit in the fall.
- Apply limestone or dolomite around any apple trees that have been showing signs of 'bitter pit' in the fruit.

MID FALL/AUTUMN

Circa April (southern hemisphere) and October (northern hemisphere

Dragonfruit and Other Fruiting Cactus
- Reduce irrigation. Do not apply fertilizer. Do not prune again until early summer.

Figs
- Protect any remaining fruit from birds etc. using organic methods suggested. Water fig trees only if there has been insufficient rain.

Stonefruit
- Water stonefruit trees only if there has been insufficient rain.

- Do not prune in cool seasons because pruning wounds take a long time to heal when the plant is not actively growing. This allows pathogens to infect the wounds.

- Pick off any mummified fruits still hanging on the trees and destroy them.

Apples
- To control apple scab, rake and destroy fallen leaves and fruit in the autumn. Pick off any mummified fruits still hanging on the trees and destroy them.

Citrus
- Inspect citrus trees for pests such as mites and treat with appropriate organic remedies.
- Apply organic manures in autumn. This allows them time to break down and release the nutrients for spring growth.

LATE FALL/AUTUMN

Circa May (southern hemisphere) and November (northern hemisphere

Berries
- Raspberries can be planted any time from late fall up until early spring before new growth begins.

Dragonfruit and Other Fruiting Cactus
- Reduce irrigation. Do not apply fertilizer. Do not prune again until early summer.

Quinces
- Brown rot is a fungal disease that causes a brown, spreading rot in fruit. Prevent the disease overwintering by removing all brown rotted quince fruit promptly, and composting. Do not allow rotted fruit to remain on the tree.

Stonefruit
- Spray with Bordeaux, copper-based fungicide or lime sulfur in autumn as leaves fall, then in winter as the flower buds swell. This controls brown rot, leaf curl, scale, mite, aphids and mealybug.
- Do not prune in the fall or winter.
- Keep an eye on the lower bark and branches for mice or rabbit injury; if this is a problem, you may need to install tree guards or fence in young trees with chicken wire for the winter.

Apples
- Rake and destroy fallen leaves and fruit.

Citrus
- Apply organic manures in autumn. This allows them time to break down and release the nutrients for spring growth.

Index

A

All-round insecticide 206
American gooseberry mildew 85
Anthracnose 4, 71–283
Apples and crabapples 55
  apple scab 56
  brown rot 61
  codling moth 59
  light brown apple moth 61
  powdery mildew 59
  wooly aphid 63
Apricots, 181–283
Attracting beneficial predators 200
Attracting beneficial predators
  carrot family 200
  daisy family 201
  ladybeetle feeder 202
  mint family 201
Avocado 68

B

Bacterial canker 148
Bacterial spot 149
Bacterial stem rot 99
Bananas 69
  banana aphid 76
  Banana bunchy top virus 70
  banana flower thrips 77
  banana fruit caterpillar 77
  banana leaf speckle 72
  banana leaf rust 71
  banana rust thrips 78
  banana scab moth 78
  banana-silvering thrips 78
  banana-spotting bug 74
  banana weevil borer 78
  burrowing nematode 75
  cluster caterpillar 79
  crown rot 72
  fruit speckle 73
  Panama disease 70
  sugarcane bud moth 81
  yellow sigatoka 73
Barriers 207
Beer trap for snails and slugs 207
Beneficial amphibians 199
Beneficial arachnids 198
  Spiders 198
Beneficial birds 200
Beneficial insects 49, 50, 64, 161, 162, 182, 197, 198, 200, 201, 214, 216, 217–283
  green lacewings 197
  ladybeetles 197–283
Beneficial insects
  hoverflies 197
  praying mantises 197
  predatory mites 198
  robber flies 198
Beneficial predators 19, 48, 195, 196, 201, 209–283
Beneficial predators

aphelinus mali 63
attracting benefical predators 200
beneficial amphibians 199
beneficial arachnids 198
beneficial birds 200
beneficial insects 197
beneficial reptiles 199
Beneficial reptiles
　beneficial reptiles 199
　Garden Skinks 199
Berries 83
　American gooseberry mildew 85
　birds 95–283
　blueberry leaf rust 92
　caterpillars 94–283
　currant borer moth 85
　currant leaf spot 94
　flying foxes 95–283
　mildew 93–283
　raspberry botrytis 88
　raspberry cane spot 87
　scale 95–283
　spur blight 90
Bicarbonate fungicide 210
Birds 6
Blackcurrants 85, 93, 256–283
Black peach aphid 149, 182
Black spot 170
Blossom blight 150
Blossom drop 103–283
Blueberries 92, 244, 248, 256–283
Blueberry leaf rust 92
Bordeaux mixture 209, 215–283
Bronze-orange bugs 114–283
Brown rot 152
Brown soft scale 104, 105–283
Brown spot 105–283
Bryobia mite 153
Bunch mite 134

C

Cactus fruit 97
  bacterial stem rot 99
  fungal stem rot 100
Carob moth 153
Carrot family 200
Caterpillar control 216
Caterpillars 8, 20, 77, 94, 126, 127, 128, 129, 200, 206, 208, 213–283
Cherries 25, 181, 183, 184, 186–283
Cherry fruitworm 183
Chilli spray 206
Citrus canker 106–283
Citrus care 218
Citrus collar rot 107–283
Citrus fruits 101
  black spot 103–283
  blossom drop 103–283
  bronze-orange bugs 114–283
  brown soft scale 104–283
  brown spot 105–283
  citrus canker 106–283
  citrus collar rot 107–283
  citrus gall wasp 108–283
  citrus leafminer 110–283
  citrus thrips 112–283
  citrus whitefly 113–283
  melanose 115–283
  soft brown rot 113–283
  sooty mold 114–283
  spined citrus bugs 114
Citrus gall wasp 108–283
Citrus leafminer 110, 111, 112–283
Citrus thrips 112–283
Citrus whitefly 112, 113–283
Cockroach control 216
Codling moth 8, 9, 10, 59, 174, 175, 192, 193, 193, 193, 238, 244–283
Codling moth control 216
Coffee Spray 206
Collar rot 184
Commercial organic remedies 213

Copper 5, 8, 48, 60, 62, 88, 89, 92, 107, 115, 117, 122, 154, 157, 172, 178, 184, 185, 209, 215, 227, 230, 232, 235, 240, 259-283
Copper fungicide 88, 227, 232-283
Copper hydroxide 92-283
Crop protection
  netting 6, 16, 20, 29, 30, 36, 38, 95, 138, 235, 237, 243, 247, 249, 251, 255-283
Crown gall 154
Curly leaf 184
Currant borer moth 85
Currant leaf spot 94
Currants
  currant borer moth 85
  currant leaf spot 94

D

Deterrent: bird, flying fox and possum 216
Diatomaceous earth 217
Diseases
  banana bunchy top virus 70
  banana leaf rust 71
  banana leaf speckle 72
  crown gall 154
  fig mosaic virus 121
  Panama disease 70
  pawpaw mosaic virus 170
Dried fruit beetle 120

E

Earwigs 11
Elephant weevil 140
European red mite 14, 155
Exclusion 218

F

Fertilizer
  granite meal 224
  greensand 224
  kelp meal 224

potash 4, 26, 104, 118, 171, 231, 233, 236–283
Fig blister mite 121
Fig fruit drop 122
Fig longicorn borer 140
Fig mosaic virus 121
Fig rust 122–283
Figs 119
   dried fruit beetle 120
   fig blister mite 121
   fig fruit drop 122
   fig mosaic virus 121
   fig rust 122–283
   root-knot nematode 123–283
Fleck 192
Flying foxes 95–283
Fruit canker 144
Fruit Care Almanac
      - fall 253
      - spring 229
      - summer 239
      - winter 221
Fruit fly 32–261, 33–261, 34–261, 35–261, 36–261, 74–261, 80–261,
    102–261, 123–261, 160–261, 192–261, 193–261, 234–261, 237–261,
    242–261, 243–261, 247–261, 250–261, 251–261
Fruit fly control 216
Fruit fly resistant fruits 36
Fruit fly traps 34
Fruit piercing moth 15
Fruit-tree borer 141
Fungal control 218
Fungal diseases
  American gooseberry mildew 85
  anthracnose 4, 71, 120, 170, 171–283
  apple scab 56
  bacterial canker 148
  bacterial spot 149
  bacterial stem rot 99
  black spot 103–283
  black spot 170
  blossom blight 150
  blueberry leaf rust 92

brown rot 61
brown spot 105–283
citrus canker 106–283
citrus collar rot 107–283
collar rot 184
crown rot 72
curly leaf 184
currant leaf spot 94
fig rust 122–283
fleck 192
fruit canker 144
fruit speckle 73
fungal diseases 94, 122, 170, 170, 170, 171, 208, 209, 210, 212, 244–283
fungal stem rot 100
grape phylloxera 126
guava anthracnose 144
hull rot 156
husk spot 157
macadamia blossom blight 151
melanose 115–283
mildew 93–283
pear scab 176
phytophthora 27, 165–283
powdery mildew 59
quince leaf blight 193
raspberry botrytis 88
raspberry cane spot 87
rust 47
scale and sooty mold 48
shothole 166
silverleaf 166, 186
soft brown rot 113–283
sooty mold 114–283
spur blight 90
strawberry black root rot 86
trunk canker 167
verticillium wilt 167, 187
walnut blight 168
yellow sigatoka 73
Fungal Diseases
  leaf blight 159–283

fungal stem rot 100
Fungicides
  sulfur spray 62
  fungicide spray 208

G

Garden skinks 199
Garlic pesticide 208
General fruit pests
      and diseases 3
General purpose organic control 217
Grapefruit 103, 110–283
Grapeleaf blister mite 133
Grapeleaf bud mite 132
Grapeleaf rust mite 134
Grape phylloxera 126
Grapes 59, 125
  bunch mite 134
  elephant weevil 140
  fig longicorn borer 140
  fruit-tree borer 141
  grapeleaf blister mite 133
  grapeleaf bud mite 132
  grapeleaf rust mite 134
  grape phylloxera 126
  grapevine hawk moth 129
  grapevine moth 128
  grapevine scale 138
  light brown apple moth 126
  mealybug 131
  mites 132–283
  nematodes 136–283
  pests of young grapevines 141
  two-spotted mite 135–283
  vine borer moth 130
  vine hawk moth 129
Grapevine hawk moth 129
Grapevine moth 128
Grapevine scale 138
Green lacewings 197

Green vegetable bug 156
Guava anthracnose 144
Guavas 143
  fruit canker 144
  guava anthracnose 144
  striped mealy bug 145–283
  wilt of guava 146–283

H

Heritage fruit ix, xvii
Homemade Bordeaux mixture 209
Homemade Burgundy mixture 209
Home-made fungicides 60
Homemade lime sulfur 211
Home made organic remedies
  all-round insecticide 206
  barriers 207
  beer trap for snails and slugs 207
  bicarbonate fungicide 210
  chilli spray 206
  coffee spray 206
  fungicide spray 208
  garlic pesticide 208
  homemade bordeaux mixture 209
  homemade burgundy mixture 209
  homemade lime sulfur 211
  horticultural oil 205
  milk fungicide 210
  molasses spray 208
  orange peel earwig trap 208
  pawpaw spray 206
  potassium soap spray 207
  salt and vinegar weedkiller 209
  soap spray 206
  spraying equipment 212
  usage 213
  vegetable oil and soy sauce trap 207
  vinegar algae killer 210
  white oil 205
  yeast spray 209

Horticultural glues 218
Horticultural oil 205
Hoverflies 197
Hull rot 156
Husk spot 157

I

Indian meal moth 158
Iron deficiency 116, 118–283

L

Ladybeetle feeder 202
Ladybeetles 197–283. *See also* Ladybirds, ladybugs
Leaf blight 159, 193–283
Light brown apple moth 126
Lime sulfur 214

M

Macadamia blossom blight 151
Macadamia felted coccid 162
Macadamia flower caterpillar 160
Macadamia leafminer 161
Macadamia nutborer 159
Macadamia twig-girdler 163
Magnesium 117, 118–283
Mandarins 103, 108–283
Manganese 117, 232–283
Mealybug 131
Melanose 115, 225, 232–283
Mildew 59, 60, 85, 93, 94, 210, 212, 214, 215, 226, 234, 236, 238, 244–283
Milk fungicide 210
Mineral-based organic pesticides 214
Mites 14, 15, 51, 53, 54, 99, 121, 132, 132, 132, 133, 134, 135, 136, 164, 165, 179, 198, 205, 206, 207, 214, 217, 226, 232, 235, 238, 244, 252, 256, 258, 283
Molasses spray 208

N

Natural enemies 127
Nectarines, xv, 181
Neem 13, 88, 213, 218, 218, 218–283
Nematodes 41, 42, 43, 44, 45, 46, 47, 75, 76, 122, 123, 136, 137, 138, 163, 208, 280, 281, 282, 283
Nitrogen deficiency 116–283
Nutritional deficiencies 103, 116–283
Nuts 147
  bacterial canker 148
  bacterial spot 149
  banana-spotting bug 149
  black peach aphid 149
  blossom blight 150
  brown rot 152
  bryobia mite 153
  carob moth 153
  crown gall 154
  European red mite 155
  green vegetable bug 156
  hull rot 156
  husk spot 157
  Indian meal moth 158
  leaf blight 159–283
  macadamia blossom blight 151
  macadamia felted coccid 162
  macadamia flower caterpillar 160
  macadamia leafminer 161
  macadamia nutborer 159
  macadamia twig-girdler 163
  peach silver mite 164
  phytophthora 165–283
  rust 165–283
  rust mite 165
  san jose scale 166–283
  scale insects 163
  shothole 166
  silverleaf 166
  trunk canker 167
  two-spotted spider mite 167–283

verticillium wilt 167–283
walnut blight 168

O

Orange peel earwig trap 208
Oranges 103, 108–283
Organic fungicides 60, 73, 103, 115, 178, 238, 244–283
Organic fungicides
  copper based fungicide 5, 172–283
Organic pesticide enhancer 215

P

Pawpaw mosaic virus 170
Pawpaws 169
  anthracnose 170
  black spot 170
  fungal diseases 170–283
  grasshoppers 172
  pawpaw mosaic virus 170
  possums 172
  rats 172
Pawpaw spray 206
Peaches xv, 11, 41, 181, 184, 185, 187–283
Peach silver mite 164
Pear and cherry slug 25, 26, 192, 193, 193, 231, 241–283
Pear leaf blister mite 179
Pears 173
  codling moth 174
  european red mite 174
  mealybugs 174
  oriental fruit moth 174
  pear leaf blister mite 179
  pear scab 176
  San Jose scale 179
  thrips 179
  two-spotted mite 179
Pest and disease remedies 205
  home made organic remedies 205
Pests
  avocado red mite 68

INDEX

banana aphid 76
banana flower thrips 77
banana fruit caterpillar 77
banana rust thrips 78
banana scab moth 78
banana-silvering thrips 78
banana-spotting bug 74
banana weevil borer 78
birds 6
black peach aphid 149, 182
bronze-orange bugs 114–283
brown soft scale 104–283
bryobia mite 153
bunch mite 134
burrowing nematode 75
carob moth 153
caterpillars 94–283
cherry fruitworm 183
citrus gall wasp 108–283
citrus leafminer 110–283
citrus thrips 112–283
citrus whitefly 113–283
cluster caterpillar 79
codling moth 8, 59, 193–283
currant borer moth 85
dried fruit beetle 120
earwigs 11
elephant weevil 140
European red mite 14, 155
fig blister mite 121
fig longicorn borer 140
fruit fly 193–261
fruit piercing moth 15
fruit-piercing moth 80
fruit-spotting bug, 16, 68
fruit-tree borer 141
grapeleaf blister mite 133
grapeleaf bud mite 132
grapeleaf rust mite 134
grapevine hawk moth 129
grapevine moth 128

grapevine scale 138
grasshoppers 18
green vegetable bug 156
Indian meal moth 158
light brown apple moth 20, 61, 126
macadamia felted coccid 162
macadamia flower caterpillar 160
macadamia leafminer 161
macadamia nutborer 159
macadamia twig-girdler 163
mealybug 22, 131
mirid bug 24, 68
mites 132–283
nematodes 136–283
peach silver mite 164
pear and cherry slug 25, 193–283
pear leaf blister mite 179
pests of young grapevines 141
possums 28
Queensland fruit fly 32, 80
rabbits 37
rats 39
root-knot nematode 41, 123–283
rust mite 165
San Jose scale 52, 166–283
scale 95–283
scale and sooty mold 48
scale insects 163, 185
spined citrus bugs 114
striped mealy bug 145–283
sugarcane bud moth 81
thrips 52
two-spotted mite 53, 135–283
two-spotted spider mite 80, 167–283
vine borer moth 130
vine hawk moth 129
wooly aphid 63
Pests of young grapevines 141
pH 26, 84, 116, 168, 171, 231, 241–283
Pheremones 127–283
Phosphorus deficiency 116–283

Phytophthora 27, 28, 165, 167–283
Piperonyl butoxide 215–283
Plant based organic insecticides 213
Plums, 25, 181–283
Potassium 48, 60, 117, 171, 205, 206, 207, 217, 218, 224, 225, 231, 232, 233, 234, 236, 237, 240, 241, 242, 243, 246, 247, 249, 250, 252, 254, 255, 257–283
Potassium Soap Spray 207
Praying Mantises 197
Predatory insects 26, 48, 135, 200–283
Predatory mites 198
Pyrethrins 213–283
Pyrethrum 213, 214, 219–283

Q

Quince leaf blight 193
Quinces 191
  codling moth 193–283
  fleck 192
  fruit fly 193–261
  pear and cherry slug 193–283
  quince leaf blight 193

R

Raspberry botrytis 88
Raspberry cane spot 87
Robber flies 198
Root-knot nematode 44, 46, 123, 281–283
Rootstock 64–283
Rust 47, 48, 68, 71, 78, 92, 122, 134, 135, 136, 165, 232–283
Rust mite 165

S

Salt and vinegar weedkiller 209
San Jose scale 51, 166, 179–283
Scale x, 25, 48, 49, 50, 51, 52, 95, 104, 105, 114, 138, 139, 163, 166, 179, 182, 185, 205, 222, 224, 226, 227, 235, 237, 238, 243, 245, 256, 259–283
Scale insects 49, 95, 163, 185, 185–283
Shothole 166

Silverleaf 166, 186
Slug and snail control 219
Soap spray 206
Soft brown rot 113-283
Sooty mold 22, 48, 49, 63, 76, 104, 113, 114, 131, 139, 182, 210, 237, 243-283
Spiders 198, 9, 18, 26, 33, 51, 127, 135, 176, 198-283
Spined citrus bugs 114
Spraying equipment 212
Spur blight 90
Sticky garden traps 219
Stonefruit 181
  black peach aphid 182
  cherry fruitworm 183
  collar rot 184
  curly leaf 184
  scale insects 185
  silverleaf 186
  verticillium wilt 187
Strawberries 59
  strawberry black root rot 86
Striped mealy bug 145-283
Sulfur 214

T

Trade names of some organic remedies 216
Trunk canker 167
Two-spotted mite 53, 135, 179-283
Two-spotted spider mite 167, 167-283

V

Vegetable oil and soy sauce trap 207
Verticillium wilt 167, 187, 187-283
Vine borer moth 130
Vinegar algae killer 210
Vine hawk moth 129

W

Walnut blight 168
Wasp control 219
Watering 27, 64, 76, 91, 103, 110, 118, 148, 223, 224, 243, 245, 247, 250, 251, 255–283
Weed control 219
White oil 64–283
White oil 205

Y

Yeast spray 209

Z

Zinc 58, 117, 232–283

Some Heritage Fruit Groups in Australia

Werribee Park Heritage Orchard, situated near Melbourne, Australia, is a beautiful antique orchard dating from the 1870s, on the grounds of the old mansion by the Werribee River. It was renowned for its peaches, grapes, apples, quinces, pears, a variety of plums and several other fruits, as well as walnuts and olives. Recently this historic treasure has been rediscovered. Volunteers are replanting and tending the orchard.

www.werribeeparkheritageorchard.org.au

The Heritage Fruits Society is also based in Melbourne, Australia. Their aim is to conserve heritage fruit varieties on private and public land. They enable and encourage society members to research this wide range of varieties and to inform the public on the benefits of heritage fruits for health, sustainability and biodiversity.

www.heritagefruitssociety.org.au

The Heritage and Rare Fruit Network's purpose is to provide a forum for sharing information on all varieties of fruit and less common useful plants, to link up people with an interest in growing unusual fruit, and to support sharing of propagation material through grafting days and any other means.

heritageandrarefruits.weebly.com

The Rare Fruit Society of South Australia is an amateur organisation of fruit tree growers who preserve heritage varieties, explore climate limitations and study propagation, pruning and grafting techniques.

www.rarefruit-sa.org.au

MARIGOLD REFERENCES

Alam, M. M., Saxena, S. K., and Khan, A. M. 1978. Suitability of crops to certain ectoparasitic nematodes. Acta Botanical Indica 6 (supplement): 205-208.

Arnason, J. T. B., J. R. Philogene, P. Morand, K. Imrie, S. Iyengar, F. Duval, C. Soucy-Breau, J. C. Scaiano, N. H. Werstiuk, B. Hasspieler, and A. E. R. Downe. 1989. Naturally occurring and synthetic thiophenes as photoactivated insecticides. ACS Symposium Series 387: 164-172.

Belcher, J. V. and R. S. Hussey. 1977. Influence of Tagetes patula and Arachis hypogaea on Meloidogyne incognita. Plant Disease Reporter 61: 525-528.

Carpenter, A. S., and S. A. Lewis. 1991. Aggressiveness and reproduction of four Meloidogyne arenaria populations on soybean. Journal of Nematology 23: 232-238.

Caswell, E. P., J. deFrank, W. J. Apt, and C.-S. Tang. 1991. Influence of nonhost plants on population decline of Rotylenchulus reniformis. Journal of Nematology 23: 91-98.

Crow W. T. 2003/5. Nematode Management for Bedding Plants, Entomology and Nematology Department, Florida Cooperative Extension Service, Institute of Food and Agricultural Sciences, University of Florida, Gainesville, FL., ENY-052, http://edis.ifas.ufl.edu/IN470.

Doubrava, N. and J. H. Blake. 1999. Root-knot nematodes in the vegetable garden. Publication number HGIC 2216. Home and Garden Information Center, Clemson University, Cooperative Extension Service, Clemson, SC. http://www.clemson.edu/extension/hgic/pests/plant_pests/veg_fruit/hgic2216.html. accessed 03-07-2007

Dover K. E., McSorley R., Wang K. -H, 2003. Marigolds as cover crops, http://agroecology. ifas.ufl.edu/Marigoldsbackground.htm accessed 06-12-2007.

El-Hamawi, M. H., Youssef, M. M. A., Zawam, H.S. 2004.

Management of Meloidogyne incognita, the root-knot nematode, on soybean as affected by marigold and sea ambrosia (damsisa) plants, J Pest Sci 77: 95-98.

Evenhuis, A., Korthals, G.W., Molendijk, L.P.G., 2004. Tagetes patula as an effective catch crop for long-term control of Pratylenchus penetrans, Nematology, Vol. 6(6), 877-881.

Geo. W. Park Seed Co., Inc. 2007. Flowers and Vegetables. Spring 2007. p. 46-47.

Gommers, F. J. and J. Bakker. 1988. Physiological diseases induced by plant responses or products. Pp. 3-22 in: Diseases of nematodes. G. O. Poinar, Jr. and H. -B. Jansson, eds., Vol. I. CRC Press, Inc., Boca Raton, FL.

Hethelyi, E., B. Danos, and P. Tetenyi. 1986. GC-MS analysis of the essential oils of four Tagetes species and the anti-microbial activity of Tagetes minuta. Flavor and Fragrance Journal 1: 169-173.

Khan, A. M., S. K. Saxena, and Z. A. Siddiqi. 1971. Efficacy of Tagetes erecta in reducing root infesting nematodes of tomato and okra. Indian Phytopathology 24: 166-169.

R. Krueger, K. E. Dover, R. McSorley (retired), Entomology and Nematology Department, Institute of Food and Agricultural Sciences, University of Florida, Gainesville, FL 32611; and K. -H. Wang, Department of Plant and Environmental Protection Services, University of Hawaii at Manoa, Honolulu, HI 96822.

Ko, M. P., and D. P. Schmitt. 1993. Pineapple inter-cycle crops to reduce plant-parasitic nematode populations. Acta Horticulturae 334: 373-382.

Lehman, P. S. 1979. Factors influencing nematode control with marigolds. Nematology Circular No. 50. Florida Department of Agriculture and Consumer Services, Division of Plant Industry, Gainesville, FL.

Marles, R. J., J. B. Hudson, E. A. Graham, C. S. -Breau, P. Morand, R. L. Compadre, C. M. Compadre, G. H. N. Towers, and J. T. Arnason. 1992. Structure-activity studies of photoactivated antiviral and cytotoxic thiophenes. Phytochemistry and Phytobiology 56: 479-487.

McSorley, R., M. Ozores-Hampton, P. A. Stansly, and J. M. Conner. 1999. Nematode management, soil fertility, and yield in organic vegetable production. Nematropica 29: 205-213.

Motsinger, R. E., E. H. Moody, and C. M. Gay. 1977. Reaction of certain French marigold (Tagetes patula) cultivars to three Meloidogyne spp. Journal of Nematology 9: 278.

Ploeg, A. T. 2000. Effects of amending soil with Tagetes patula cv. Single Gold on Meloidogyne incognita infestation on tomato. Nematology 2: 489-493.

Ploeg, A. T. and P. C. Maris. 1999. Effect of temperature on suppression of Meloidogyne incognita by Tagetes cultivars. Journal of Nematology 31(4S): 709-714.

Powers, L. E., R. McSorley, and R. A. Dunn. 1993. Effects of mixed cropping on a soil nematode community in Honduras. Journal of Nematology 25: 666-673.

Pudasaini, M.P., Viaene, N., Moens, M. 2006. Effect of marigold (Tagetes patula) on population dynamics of Pratylenchus penetrans in a field, Nematology, Vol. 8 (4): 477-484.

Rhoades, H. L. 1980. Relative susceptibility of Tagetes patula and Aeschynomene americana to plant nematodes in Florida, USA. Nematropica 10: 116-120.

Rickard, D. A., and A. W. DuPree, Jr. 1978. The effectiveness of ten kinds of marigolds and five other treatments for control of four Meloidogyne spp. Journal of Nematology 4: 296-297.

Siddiqui, M. A. and M. M. Alam. 1988. Toxicity of different plant parts of Tagetes lucida to plant parasitic nematodes. Indian Journal of Nematology 18: 181-185.

Soule, J. 1993. Tagetes minuta: A potential new herb from South America. Pp. 649-654 in: Janick, J. and J. E. Simon (eds.), New Crops, Wiley, NY. http://www.hort.purdue.edu/newcrop/proceedings1993/ v2-649.html#BOTANY.

Suatmadji, R. W. 1969. Studies on the effect of Tagetes species on plant parasitic nematodes. Stichting Frond Landbouw Export Bureau publicatie 47. H. Veenman Und Zonen N. V., Wageningen, Netherlands. 132p.

Tyler, J. 1938. Proceedings of the root-knot conferences held at Atlanta. Plant Disease Reporter Supplement 109: 133-151.

Vann, S., T. Kirkpatrick, and R. Cartwright. 2003. Control root-knot nematodes in your garden. Publication number FSA7529-PD-5-02N. Division of Agriculture, University of Arkansas, Cooperative Extension Service, Little Rock, AR.

DeWaele, D., E. M. Jordaan, and S. Basson. 1990. Host status of seven weed species and their effects on Ditylenchus destructor infestation of peanut. Journal of Nematology 22: 292-296.

Wang, K.-H., B. S. Sipes, and D. P. Schmitt. 2001. Suppression of Rotylenchulus reniformis by Crotalaria juncea, Brassica napus, and Tagetes erecta, Nematropica 31: 237-251.

Wang, K.-H., B. S. Sipes, and D. P. Schmitt. 2002. Management of Rotylenchulus reniformis in pineapple, Ananas comosus, by intercycle cover crops. Journal of Nematology 34: 106-114.

Wang, K.-H., B. S. Sipes, and D. P. Schmitt. 2003. Intercropping cover crops with pineapple for the management of Rotylenchulus reniformis. Journal of Nematology 35: 39-47.

Winfield, A. L. 1985. Observations of the pin nematodes, Pratylenchus nanus, a possible pest of glasshouse lettuce, Lactuca sativa. Crop Research (Edinburgh) 25: 3-12.

Printed in Great Britain
by Amazon